Intr

I recently purchased an air fryer and to cook healthier meals. However, I soon discovered that there was a real lack of decent air fryer recipe books. Therefore, as an author of a few recipes books, I decided to try and put together the most complete air fryer recipe cookbook. The intention of the book is to provide simple, delicious and low calorie air fryer recipes. This book provides a list of recipes for starters, sides, main courses and desserts. Therefore, I refer to it as a complete cookbook and not just a list of random recipes. Please note that eggs are included in some of these recipes. I am aware that certain people are against eating eggs. Therefore, you need to use your discretion and decide if this book is for you. Supermarket eggs are unfertilized and I do not consider them to be a meat product. Consulting this book will provide clear instructions on what ingredients to use and the method to go about making the meal. The Airfryer temperature and time settings are given with each recipe. Certain recipes require additional equipment to make. Images are included with all recipes. This is to ensure that you have an idea of what the completed dish should look like.

Legal Notes

Contents

Starters and Snacks

Thai Fish Cakes with Mango Salsa

Servings 4 persons, Preparation time 20 minutes, Cooking time: 14 minutes

Ingredients

- 1 ripe mango
- 1½ teaspoons red chili paste
- 3 tablespoons fresh coriander or flat leaf parsley
- Juice and zest of 1 lime
- 500 g white fish fillet (cod, tilapia, pangasius, pollack)
- 1 egg
- 1 green onion, finely chopped
- 50 g ground coconut

Directions

1. Peel the mango and cut it into small cubes. Mix the mango cubes in a bowl with ½ teaspoon red chili paste, 1 tablespoon coriander and the juice and zest of half a lime.
2. Purée the fish in the food processor and then mix with 1 egg and 1 teaspoon salt and the remainder of the lime zest, red chili paste and the lime juice. Mix with the remainder of the coriander, the green onion and 2 tablespoons coconut.
3. Put the remainder of the coconut on a soup plate. Divide the fish mixture into 12 portions, shape them into round cakes and coat them with the coconut.
4. Place six fish cakes in the basket and slide it into the Airfryer. Preheat the Airfryer to 200°C.
5. Set the timer to 7 minutes and fry the fish cakes until they are golden brown and done. Fry the remainder of the fish cakes in the same way.
6. Serve the fish cakes with the mango salsa. Good with pandan rice and stir-fried pak choi.

Salmon Croquettes

Servings 2 persons, Preparation time 10 minutes, Cooking time: 10 minutes

Ingredients

- 1 (180g) tin salmon, drained and flaked
- 1 egg
- 4 tablespoons finely chopped celery
- 4 tablespoons sliced spring onion
- 1 tablespoon chopped fresh dill
- 1/2 teaspoon garlic granules
- 5 tablespoons wheat germ
- 3 tablespoons olive oil

Directions

1. In a medium bowl, mix together the salmon, egg, celery, green onion, dill and garlic granules. Form the mixture into golf ball size, and roll in wheat germ to coat.

2. Preheat the Airfryer to 200 °C. Flatten the balls slightly, and fry for about 7 minutes, turning as needed, until golden brown.

Roasted Pepper Rolls

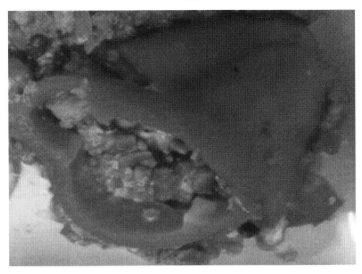

Servings 8 persons, Preparation time 25 minutes, Cooking time: 10 minutes

Ingredients

- 2 medium-sized red, yellow and/or orange bell peppers, halved
- Filling as desired

Directions

1. Preheat the Airfryer to 200°C.
2. Put the bell peppers in the basket and slide the basket into the Airfryer. Set the timer to 10 minutes and roast the peppers until the skin is slightly roasted to a charred nature.
3. Halve the bell peppers lengthwise and remove the seeds and the skin.
4. Coat the bell pepper pieces with a filling of your choice and roll them up, starting from the narrowest end.
5. Secure the rolls with tapas forks and put them in a platter.
6. Fillings - Anchovy with Capers Drain a tin of anchovy fillets and finely chop the fillets. Mix the anchovy fillets with one crushed clove of garlic, 2 tablespoons of finely chopped capers, 2 tablespoons finely

chopped parsley and some freshly ground black pepper. - Feta with green onion Crumble 100g Greek feta cheese and mix it with one thinly sliced green onion and 2 tablespoons finely chopped oregano. - Tuna with Red Onion Drain one tin of tuna in olive oil and mix the tuna with one finely chopped red onion, 1 tablespoon grated lemon peel, 2 tablespoons of capers, salt and freshly ground black pepper to taste.

Roast Paprika Potatoes with Greek Yoghurt

Servings 4 persons, Preparation time 10 minutes, Cooking time: 20 minutes

Ingredients

- 800 g waxy potatoes
- 2 tablespoons olive oil
- 1 tablespoon spicy paprika
- Freshly ground black pepper
- 150 ml Greek yoghurt

Directions

1. Preheat the Airfryer to 180°C. Peel the potatoes and cut them into 3 cm cubes. Soak the cubes in water for at least 30 minutes. Drain them thoroughly and then pat them dry with kitchen paper.
2. In a medium-sized bowl, mix 1 tablespoon olive oil with the paprika and add pepper to taste. Coat the potato cubes with the spicy oil.
3. Transfer the potato cubes to the fryer basket and slide the basket into the Airfryer. Set the timer to 20 minutes and fry the potato cubes until they are golden brown and done. Turn them every now and again.

4. Mix the Greek yoghurt in a small bowl with the remaining spoonful of olive oil and add salt and pepper to taste. Sprinkle with paprika. Serve the yoghurt as a dip with the potatoes.
5. Serve the potato cubes in a platter and sprinkle with salt. Goes well with with a rib eye or with kebabs.

Roast Potatoes with Tuna

Servings 2 persons, Preparation time 10 minutes, Cooking time: 30 minutes

Ingredients

- 4 starchy potatoes, approximately 125 g each
- ½ tablespoon olive oil
- 1 can of tuna in oil, drained
- 2 tablespoons (Greek) yoghurt
- 1 teaspoon chili powder
- 1 green onion, finely sliced into rings
- Freshly ground black pepper
- 1 tablespoon capers

Directions

1. Preheat the Airfryer to 180°C. Soak the potatoes for at least 30 minutes and pat them dry with kitchen paper.
2. Lightly brush the potatoes with olive oil and place them in the fryer basket. Slide the basket into the Airfryer and set the timer to 30 minutes to fry the potatoes until they are crunchy and done.

3. In a bowl, finely mash the tuna and add the yoghurt and chili powder. Mix well. Stir in half of the green onion and season to taste with salt and pepper.
4. Place the potatoes on two plates and cut the top side lengthwise. Slightly push the potato open and spoon the tuna mixture onto the open potato. Sprinkle the filling with chili powder and spoon the capers and the rest of the green onion on top. Good with a fresh salad.

Risotto Balls

Servings 9 persons, Preparation time 30 minutes, Cooking time: 10 minutes

Ingredients

- 2 tablespoons olive oil
- 1 shallot, finely chopped
- 125 g mushrooms, chopped
- 100 g risotto rice
- 250 ml chicken stock
- 25 g freshly grated Parmesan cheese
- Freshly ground pepper
- 3 slices of stale white bread
- 1 egg

Directions

1. Heat up one tablespoon of olive oil in a thick-bottom pan and sauté the shallot. Add the mushrooms and fry until the liquid has almost evaporated.
2. Stir in the rice grains and fry until they shine. Add the stock and slow boil the rice until ready in twenty minutes.

3. Mix the cheese and parsley through the risotto and season to taste with salt and pepper.
4. Allow the risotto to cool down and refrigerate for at least one hour.
5. Grind the bread into fine crumbs in the food processor and mix in 1 tablespoon olive oil. Continue to stir until it regains a loose crumb consistency. Pour the crumbs in a deep dish.
6. Beat the eggs in another deep dish.
7. Shape the risotto into walnut-sized balls. Coat the balls in the beaten egg and then in the bread crumbs. Preheat the Airfryer to 200°C. Put 8 to 10 balls in the basket and slide the basket into the Airfryer. Set the timer to 5 minutes and bake the risotto balls until golden brown. Bake the rest of the balls in the same manner. Serve the risotto balls in a platter with red or green pesto.

Puff Pastry Nibbles

Servings 9 persons, Preparation time 10 minutes, Cooking time: 20 minutes

Ingredients

- 200 g ready-made (frozen or chilled) puff pastry
- Filling as desired
- 2 tablespoons milk

Directions

1. Preheat the Airfryer to 200°C.
2. Cut the pastry into 16 squares of 5x5 cm and scoop a heaped teaspoon of filling onto each square.
3. Fold the squares into triangles and moisten the edges with some water. Press the edges firmly together with a fork.
4. Put eight parcels in the basket and brush them with milk. Slide the basket into the Airfryer and set the timer to 10 minutes. Bake the appetizers until they are golden brown.
5. Bake the remaining parcels in the same way. Serve the puff pastry bites in a dish.

6. Fillings: - Ricotta and Ham Mix 50 g ricotta with 25 g finely-chopped ham and freshly ground pepper - Ricotta and Salmon Mix 50 g ricotta with 25 g smoked salmon and 1 tablespoon finely chopped chives - Cheese and Green Onion Mix 75 g grated cheese (Gouda, Cheddar or Gruyère) with one thinly sliced green onion - Shrimps and Dill Mix 75 g chopped pink shrimps with 1 tablespoon finely chopped dill and ½ tablespoon lemon juice - Pepper and Salami Mix 50 g salami in strips with ½ red bell pepper diced into small cubes and 1 tablespoon of finely chopped fresh oregano - Apple and Cinnamon Mix ½ apple chopped into small pieces with ½ tablespoon sugar, 1 teaspoon grated orange peel and 1 teaspoon cinnamon - Apple and Ginger Mix ½ large apple, chopped into small pieces, with 1 tablespoon finely chopped preserved ginger and 1 tablespoon of finely chopped fresh mint.

Ricotta Balls with Basil

Servings 20 persons, Preparation time 15 minutes, Cooking time: 16 minutes

Ingredients

- 250 g ricotta
- 2 tablespoons flour
- 1 egg, separated
- Freshly ground pepper
- 15 g fresh basil, finely chopped
- 1 tablespoon chives, finely chopped
- 3 slices of stale white bread

Directions

1. Mix the ricotta in a bowl with the flour, egg yolk, 1 teaspoon salt and freshly ground pepper. Stir the basil, chives and orange peel through the mixture.

2. Divide the mixture into 20 equal portions and shape them into balls with wet hands. Let them rest for a while.
3. Grind the bread slices into fine bread crumbs with the food processor and mix with the olive oil. Pour the mixture into a deep dish. Briefly beat the egg white in another deep dish.
4. Preheat the Airfryer to 200°C.
5. Carefully coat the ricotta balls in the egg white and then in the bread crumbs.
6. Put 10 balls in the basket and slide the basket into the Airfryer. Set the timer to 8 minutes. Bake the balls until golden brown. Bake the remaining balls in the same way.
7. Serve the ricotta balls in a platter.

Potato Croquettes or Salmon Croquettes

Servings 8 persons, Preparation time 15 minutes, Cooking time: 8 minutes

Ingredients

- Potato filling:
- 50 g grated parmesan cheese
- 300 g mashed potato
- 1 egg yolk
- 2 tbsp flour
- 2 tbsp finely chopped fresh chives
- nutmeg to taste
- pepper and salt to taste
- Salmon filling:
- 200 g tinned red salmon, drained
- 1 egg, lightly beaten
- 1 tbsp fresh dill, finely chopped
- 2 tbsp chives, finely chopped
- freshly ground pepper
- Breadcrumb coating:
- 2 tbsp vegetable oil
- 50 g breadcrumbs

Directions

1. Mix all of the ingredients for the potato filling together.
2. For the breadcrumb coating, mix the oil and the breadcrumbs together. Keep stirring until the mixture becomes loose and crumbly again.
3. Roll 1 tbsp of potato filling in the breadcrumbs until it is completely coated and place it in the Airfryer basket. Repeat until all the filling is used up.
4. Preheat the Airfryer to 200°C.
5. Slide the basket into the Airfryer. Set the timer for 8 minutes and fry the potato croquettes until the timer rings and they are crispy and brown.

Potato Croquettes with Parmesan Cheese

Servings 4 persons, Preparation time 30 minutes, Cooking time: 8 minutes

Ingredients

- 300 g starchy potatoes, peeled and cubed
- 1 egg yolk
- 50 g Parmesan cheese, grated
- 2 tablespoons flour
- Freshly ground pepper
- Nutmeg
- 50 g bread crumbs

Directions

1. Boil the potato cubes in salted water for 15 minutes until ready. Drain the potatoes and mash them finely with a potato masher or a ricer. Allow the mashed potatoes to cool.
2. Add the egg yolk, cheese, flour and chives to the potato puree and mix well. Season to taste with salt, pepper and nutmeg.
3. Preheat the Airfryer to 200°C. Mix the oil and the bread crumbs and keep stirring until the mixture becomes loose and crumbly again.

19

4. Shape the potato puree into 12 croquettes and roll them through the bread crumbs until they are completely coated.
5. Put six croquettes in the fryer basket and slide the basket into the Airfryer. Set the timer to 4 minutes and fry the potato croquettes until they are crispy brown. Then fry the rest of the croquettes.

Quiche Wedges

Servings 9 persons, Preparation time 10 minutes, Cooking time: 24 minutes

Ingredients

- 100 g (frozen or chilled) ready-made pie crust dough (pâte brisée)
- ½ tablespoon oil
- 1 egg
- 3 tablespoons whipping cream
- 40 g grated cheese
- Freshly ground pepper
- Filling as desired
- 2 small pie moulds of 10 cm

Directions

1. Preheat the Airfryer to 200°C.
2. Cut two rounds of 15 cm from the dough. Lightly grease the moulds with oil and line them with the dough. Press the dough down along the edges.

3. Lightly beat the egg with the cream and the cheese and season with salt and pepper to taste. Pour the mixture into the moulds and add the filling.
4. Place a mould in the basket and slide the basket into the Airfryer. Set the timer to 12 minutes. Bake the quiche until golden brown and ready. Bake the other quiche in the same way.
5. Remove the quiches from the moulds and cut each quiche into 6 wedges. Serve the quiche wedges warm or at room temperature.
6. Variations - Mushroom Slices Fry 125 g sliced mushrooms with one crushed clove of garlic and 1 teaspoon of paprika in 1 tablespoon olive oil on high heat until brown. Divide the mushrooms between the quiches. - Broccoli and Ham Slices Boil 50 g very small broccoli florets until they are tender and divide them with 50 g ham cut into strips between the quiches.

Mushroom Croquettes or Meat Croquettes

Servings 8 persons, Preparation time 15 minutes, Cooking time: 8 minutes

Ingredients

- 1/4 onion
- 100 g mushrooms
- 20 g butter
- 1½ heaped tbsp flour
- 500 ml milk
- salt
- ground nutmeg
- 2 tbsp vegetable oil
- 50 g breadcrumbs

Directions

1. Finely chop the onion and the mushrooms. Melt the butter in a saucepan and fry the onion and mushrooms. Add the flour and stir well. Warm up the milk and add it, little by little, to the mushroom mixture in the saucepan. Keep stirring until the mixture thickens. Season with salt and nutmeg to taste. Leave to cool and set for 2 hours in the refrigerator.

2. For the breadcrumb coating, mix the oil and the breadcrumbs together. Keep stirring until the mixture becomes loose and crumbly again.
3. Roll 1 tbsp of filling in the breadcrumbs until it is completely coated and place it in the Airfryer basket. Repeat until all the filling is used up.
4. Preheat the Airfryer to 200°C.
5. Slide the basket into the Airfryer. Set the timer for 8 minutes and fry the croquettes until the timer rings and they are crispy and brown.

Mini Frankfurters in Pastry

Servings 3 persons, Preparation time 10 minutes, Cooking time: 20 minutes

Ingredients

- 1 tin of mini frankfurters (drained weight 220 g, approx. 20 frankfurters)
- 100 g (chilled or frozen, defrosted) ready-made puff pastry
- 1 tablespoon fine mustard

Directions

1. Preheat the Airfryer to 200°C.
2. Thoroughly drain the sausages on a layer of kitchen paper and dab them dry.
3. Cut the puff pastry into strips measuring 5 x 1½ cm and coat the strips with a thin layer of mustard.
4. Roll each sausage spirally into a strip of pastry.
5. Put half the sausages in pastry in the basket and slide the basket into the Airfryer. Set the timer to 10 minutes. Bake the sausages in pastry

until golden brown. Bake the remaining sausages in the same manner.

6. Serve the sausages in a platter accompanied by a small dish of mustard.

Mini Peppers with Goat Cheese

Servings persons, Preparation time 10 minutes, Cooking time: 8 minutes

Ingredients

- 8 mini or snack peppers
- ½ tablespoon olive oil
- 1 teaspoon freshly ground black pepper
- 100 g soft goat cheese, in eight pieces

Directions

1. Preheat the Airfryer to 200°C.
2. Cut the top off the mini peppers and remove the seeds and membrane.
3. Mix the olive oil in a deep dish with the Italian herbs and the pepper. Toss the pieces of goat cheese in the oil.
4. Push a piece of goat cheese in each mini pepper and place the mini peppers next to each other in the basket. Slide the basket into the Airfryer and set the timer to 8 minutes. Bake the mini peppers until the cheese has melted.
5. Serve the mini peppers in small dishes as appetizers or snacks.

Empanadas with Chorizo

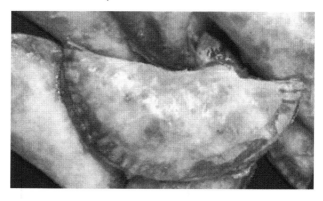

Servings persons, Preparation time 20 minutes, Cooking time: 20 minutes

Ingredients

- 125 g chorizo, in small cubes
- 1 shallot, finely chopped
- ¼ red bell pepper, diced into small cubes
- 2 tablespoons parsley
- 200 g chilled pie crust dough (pâte brisée) or pizza dough

Directions

1. Stir the chorizo with the shallot and bell pepper in a skillet and fry on low heat for 2 to 3 minutes until the bell pepper is tender. Take off the heat and stir in the parsley. Allow the mixture to cool.
2. Preheat the Airfryer to 200°C.
3. Use a glass to cut twenty 5 cm rounds from the dough. Scoop a spoonful of the chorizo mixture onto each round. Press the edges together between thumb and index finger, creating a scallop pattern.
4. Put 10 empanadas in the basket and slide the basket into the Airfryer. Set the timer to 10 minutes and bake the empanadas until they are golden brown and done.
5. Bake the remaining empanadas in the same way. Serve the empanadas lukewarm.

Meatballs with Feta

Servings 10 persons, Preparation time 10 minutes, Cooking time: 8 minutes

Ingredients

- 150 g lamb mince or lean minced beef
- 1 slice of stale white bread, turned into fine crumbs
- 50 g Greek feta, crumbled
- 1 tablespoon fresh oregano, finely chopped
- ½ tablespoon grated lemon peel
- Freshly ground black pepper
- Round, shallow oven dish, 15 cm
- Tapas forks

Directions

1. Preheat the Airfryer to 200°C.
2. Mix the mince in a bowl with the bread crumbs, feta, oregano, lemon peel and black pepper, thoroughly kneading everything together.

3. Divide the mince into 10 equal portions and form smooth balls, using damp hands.
4. Put the balls in the oven dish and place this dish in the basket. Slide the basket into the Airfryer. Set the timer to 8 minutes and bake the mince balls until they are nicely brown and done.
5. Serve the meatballs hot in a platter.

Green Salad with Roasted Pepper

Servings 4 persons, Preparation time 15 minutes, Cooking time: 10 minutes

Ingredients

- 1 red bell pepper
- 1 tablespoon lemon juice
- 3 tablespoons yoghurt
- 2 tablespoons olive oil
- Freshly ground black pepper
- 1 romaine lettuce, in broad strips
- 50 g rocket leaves

Directions

1. Preheat the Airfryer to 200°C.
2. Place the bell pepper in the basket and slide the basket into the Airfryer. Set the timer to 10 minutes and roast the bell pepper until the skin is slightly charred.

3. Put the bell pepper in a bowl and cover it with a lid or plastic wrap. Leave the bell pepper for 10-15 minutes.
4. Then cut the bell pepper into four sections and remove the seeds and the skin. Cut the bell pepper into strips.
5. Mix a dressing in a bowl, using 2 tablespoons of the moisture from the bell pepper, the lemon juice, the yoghurt, and the olive oil. Add pepper and salt to taste.
6. Toss the lettuce and the rocket leaves in the dressing, and garnish the salad with the bell pepper strips.

Garlic Mushrooms

Servings persons, Preparation time 10 minutes, Cooking time: 10 minutes

Ingredients

- 1 slice of white bread
- 1 clove garlic, crushed
- 1 tablespoon flat-leafed parsley, finely chopped
- Freshly ground black pepper
- 12 (chestnut) mushrooms

Directions

1. Preheat the Airfryer to 200°C.
2. Grind the slices of bread into fine crumbs in the food processor and mix in the garlic, parsley and some seasoning to taste. Lastly, stir in the olive oil.
3. Cut off the mushroom stalks and fill the caps with the bread crumbs.
4. Put the mushroom caps in the basket and slide it into the Airfryer. Set the timer to 10 minutes. Bake the mushrooms until crispy and golden.
5. Serve the mushrooms in a platter.

Hot Prawns with Cocktail Sauce

Servings 4 persons, Preparation time 10 minutes, Cooking time: 6 minutes

Ingredients

- 1 tsp chilli flakes
- 1 tsp chilli powder
- ½ tsp sea salt
- ½ tsp freshly ground black pepper
- 8-12 fresh king prawns
- 3 tbsp mayonnaise
- 1 tbsp ketchup
- 1 tbsp cider or wine vinegar

Directions

1. Preheat the Airfryer to 180°C.
2. Mix the spices in a bowl. Add the prawns and toss to coat them in the spices.

3. Place the spicy prawns into the Airfryer basket. Slide the basket into the Airfryer and set the timer for 6 to 8 minutes, depending on size of the prawns.
4. Mix the sauce ingredients in a bowl. Serve the hot prawns with a sauce that you prefer.

Feta Triangles

Servings 3 persons, Preparation time 20 minutes, Cooking time: 9 minutes

Ingredients

- 1 egg yolk
- 100 g feta
- 2 tablespoons flat-leafed parsley, finely chopped
- 1 green onion, finely sliced into rings
- Freshly ground black pepper
- 5 sheets of frozen filo pastry, defrosted

Directions

1. Beat the egg yolk in a bowl and mix the feta, parsley and green onion; season with pepper to taste.
2. Cut each sheet of filo pastry into three strips.
3. Scoop a full teaspoon of the feta mixture on the underside of a strip of pastry. Fold the tip of the pastry over the filling to form a triangle,

folding the strip zigzag until the filling is wrapped up in a triangle of pastry. Fill the other strips of pastry with feta in the same manner.

4. Preheat the Airfryer to 200°C.

5. Brush the triangles with a little oil and place five triangles in the basket. Slide the basket into the Airfryer and set the timer to 3 minutes. Bake the feta triangles until they are golden brown. Bake the other feta triangles in the same manner.

6. Serve the triangles in a platter.

Crispy Fried Spring Rolls

Servings 4 persons, Preparation time 20 minutes, Cooking time: 5 minutes

Ingredients

- 120 g cooked chicken breast
- 1 celery stalk
- 30 g carrot
- 30 g mushrooms
- ½ tsp fi nely chopped ginger
- 1 tsp sugar
- 1 tsp chicken stock powder
- 1 egg
- 1 tsp corn starch
- 8 spring roll wrappers

Directions

1. Tear the cooked chicken breasts into shreds. Slice the celery, carrot and mushroom into long thin strips.

2. Place the shredded chicken into a bowl and mix with the celery, carrot and mushroom. Add the ginger, sugar and chicken stock powder and stir evenly to make the spring roll filling.
3. Whisk the egg, then add the corn starch and mix to create a thick paste. Set aside.
4. Place some filling onto each spring roll wrapper and roll it up, then seal the ends with the egg mixture. For a crispy result, lightly brush the spring rolls with oil.
5. Preheat the Airfryer to 200°C.
6. Place the rolls into the Airfryer basket and slide the basket into the Airfryer. Set the timer for 4 minutes. Serve with a sauce.

Cheese Cookies

Servings 10 persons

Ingredients

For the dough:

- 180 g Gruyere cheese, grated
- 150 g margarine
- 100 ml cream
- 150 g flour
- 1 teaspoon mild paprika powder
- ½ teaspoon salt
- ½ teaspoon baking powder

To finish:

- 2 egg yolks
- 1 tablespoon milk
- Poppy seeds
- Cumin seeds
- Pistachio nuts, ground
- White and black sesame seeds
- Salt

Directions

1. Put the margarine, cheese, salt and paprika in a bowl. Pour in the cream and mix everything until smooth.
2. Sift the flour and baking powder over your work surface and make a hollow. Knead the cheese mixture into the flour and baking powder to form a dough. Knead as little as possible to prevent the dough becoming tough. If you have a food processor, you can of course use it.
3. Roll the dough out to 3-4 mm thickness and cut out cookie shapes. Mix the beaten eggs with the milk and brush the cookies. Garnish with poppy seeds, sesame seeds or salt. Place the cookies in the grill pan and bake them off in 12 minutes at 170°C.

Brown Loaf with Seeds

Servings 4 persons, Preparation time 70 minutes, Cooking time: 18 minutes

Ingredients

- 100 g whole wheat flour
- 100 g plain flour
- ½ sachet instant yeast (7 g)
- 50 g sunflower seeds and/or pumpkin seeds
- Small pizza pan or low cake pan, 15 cm diameter

Directions

1. In a bowl, mix both flours with 1 teaspoon salt, the yeast and the seeds. While stirring, add 150-200 ml lukewarm water and mix until the dough forms a soft ball.

2. Knead the dough for approximately 5 minutes until it becomes smooth and elastic. Shape the dough into a ball and place it in a bowl. Cover the bowl with plastic wrap and allow to rise in a warm place for 30 minutes.
3. Preheat the Airfryer to 200°C. Brush the top of the dough with water.
4. Put the cake pan in the fryer basket and slide the basket into the Airfryer. Set the timer to 18 minutes and bake the bread until it is golden brown and done. Allow the bread to cool on a wire rack.
5. Variations: Cheese Loaf; Use 50% whole wheat flour and 50% plain flour and replace the seeds with 50 g grated cheese. Before baking, sprinkle some cheese over the bread. Nut Loaf; Replace the seeds with coarsely chopped walnuts or hazelnuts. Make the bread with plain flour instead of whole wheat flour (optional).

Brazil Cheese Bread

Servings 8 persons

Ingredients

- 500 g tapioca flour
- 150 g milk
- 100 g Canola or sunflower oil
- 1 tablespoon salt
- 2 eggs
- 250 g strong grated cheese

Directions

1. Put the milk, cheese, oil, and eggs in a pan and bring to just below boiling point (not boiling), stirring constantly. Mix the salt with the tapioca flour, then add the warm mixture to the flour. Knead into a dough by hand or use your food processor. Make small balls of the dough and bake them in your Airfryer at 160°C for 13 minutes.
2. Use the grill pan accessory so that the balls do not stick to the basket.

Baked Mini Spinach Quiches

Servings 4 persons, Preparation time 20 minutes, Cooking time: 15 minutes

Ingredients

- 200 g flour
- 75 g butter
- 1 egg
- 2 tbsp milk
- pepper & salt
- 1 small onion
- 1 tbsp oil
- 200 g spinach
- 1 egg
- 100 g cottage cheese (unsalted)
- 4 cupcake moulds or small ramekins that fi t inside the Airfryer

Directions

1. Put all of the ingredients for the dough into a food processor with a pinch of salt and blend until you have a ball of dough. Turn out onto a worktop and knead with your hands until you have a smooth dough. Leave to rest in the refrigerator for 15 minutes.

45

2   Finely chop the onion. Heat the oil in a pan and add the onion. Sweat until translucent, then add the spinach and fry for 1 to 2 minutes more until the spinach is wilted. In a bowl, whisk the egg and stir in the cottage cheese.

3   Squeeze the excess water out of the spinach, chop and add to the cheese mixture.

4   Divide the dough into 4 equal parts. Roll each part into a round, large enough to cover the bottom of the moulds. Line the moulds with the dough. Fill each mould with the spinach filling.

5   Preheat the Airfryer to 180°C. Place the quiche(s) into the Airfryer basket and slide the basket into the Airfryer. Set the timer for 15 minutes. Serve the quiches lukewarm or cold.

6   You can also make a large spinach quiche. In that case, use double the dough to line a 20 cm spring form, and fill with double the filling. Bake for 20-25 minutes.

Sides

French Fries

Servings 4 persons

Ingredients

- 800 g potatoes, peeled
- Oil of choice

Directions

1. Peel the potatoes and slice into neat fries. Place the sliced potatoes in cold water for half an hour. Blot dry with a clean towel.
2. Put the fries in a bowl and add a spoonful of oil. Mix well.
3. Preheat the oven and place the fries in the Airfryer. The cooking time for a regular Airfryer is 30 minutes at 190°C.

Roasted Asian Chicken Wings

Servings 4 persons, Preparation time 5 min, Cooking time: 10 min

Ingredients

- 2 cloves garlic
- 1 teaspoon ground cumin
- 500 g chicken wings at room temperature
- 2 teaspoons ginger powder
- Freshly ground black pepper
- 100 ml sweet chili sauce

Directions

1. Preheat the Airfryer to 180°C.
2. Mix the garlic with the ginger powder, cumin, plenty of freshly ground black pepper and some salt. Rub the chicken wings with the herbs.

48

3. Put the chicken wings in the basket and slide it into the Airfryer. Set the timer to 10 minutes and roast the chicken wings until they are crispy brown.
4. Serve the chicken wings with the chili sauce as a main course or a snack.

Mediterranean Quinoa Salad

Servings 6 persons

Ingredients

- 130 g quinoa
- 50 g olives, preferably Kalamata
- 2 tablespoons capers
- 150 g sundried tomatoes
- 200 g roasted bell peppers
- 400 g kidney beans
- 1 green chili pepper
- 200 g chicken breast
- 2 garlic cloves
- 1 red onion
- 2 tablespoons chives
- 3 tablespoons dill
- 1 chicken bouillon cube
- 14 anchovy fillets
- 2 tablespoons red wine vinegar

Directions

1. Cut the chicken into small strips and fill the SoupMaker with the quinoa and chicken meat. Add one bouillon cube and fill with water to the lower line. Now Select program 3 on the SoupMaker.
2. Once the program is finished, leave the SoupMaker shut for another 15 minutes so that the quinoa can cook. Meanwhile, de-stone the olives, finely chop the red onion and cut the sun-dried tomato into small strips.
3. Rinse the kidney beans and drain them well. Grill the bell peppers in the Airfryer and remove the skin. If you're using roasted peppers from a jar, rinse them briefly. Cut the bell peppers into strips. Prepare the chili pepper and finely chop together with the chives and dill. Crush the garlic. Mix all the ingredients in a bowl and add the capers and anchovies. Dress the salad to taste with the red wine vinegar, olive oil and salt and pepper.
4. The salad should be served a little warmer than 'chilled'.

Hornazo

Servings 6 person

Ingredients

For the dough:

- 500 g flour
- 125 g water
- 125 g milk
- 35 g fresh yeast
- 1 teaspoon salt
- 200 g ground meat (half beef, half pork)
- 200 g chorizo
- 4 boiled eggs
- 1 garlic clove
- 1 tablespoon chopped parsley
- 1 egg, lightly beaten

Directions

1. Heat the milk until it is lukewarm. Dissolve the yeast in the milk and make a smooth bread dough from the rest of the ingredients. If you

have a food processor, you can create a smooth dough with the dough hook. Put the dough in a bowl and leave for at least 1.5 hours to rise under a damp, warm cloth.

2. Meanwhile, peel the garlic and peel the onions. Chop everything finely and mix this with the minced meat, the parsley and the egg to create the filling. Boil the eggs hard and peel them.

3. Take the dough out of the bowl and roll it out to the size of the grill pan. Keep a small ball of dough to one side to decorate the Hornazo with. If you have a regular sized Airfryer, I suggest you divide the dough in two and bake in two batches because the Airfryer is a little smaller.

4. Place the filling on the dough in one piece and top with the chorizo and eggs. Coat the edges of the dough with the beaten egg and fold shut. Let rise for 30 minutes. Meanwhile, roll out the remaining dough and cut out shapes.

5. Make a small hole in the bread and create a little chimney from aluminum foil. This will allow the air to escape during baking. Decorate the bread with the dough shapes. Brush the bread with lightly beaten egg and bake the Hornazo for 45 minutes at 150°C.

Courgette Gratin

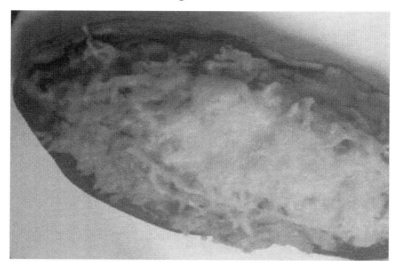

Servings 4 persons, Preparation time 10 minutes, Cooking time: 15 minutes

Ingredients

- 2 courgettes
- 1 tbsp chopped fresh parsley
- 2 tbsp breadcrumbs
- 4 tbsp grated cheese
- 1 tbsp oil
- Pepper

Directions

1. Preheat the Airfryer to 180°C.
2. Slice the courgettes in half lengthways and cut each piece in half again through the middle. You'll end up with 8 pieces of courgette. Place into the Airfryer basket.
3. Mix together the parsley, breadcrumbs, cheese, oil and freshly ground black pepper to taste.

4. Top the courgette with the mixture. Slide the basket into the Airfryer and set the timer for 15 minutes. Fry the courgette gratin until the timer rings and the gratin is golden brown.

Breakfast Soufflé Special

Servings 2 persons

Ingredients

- 2 eggs
- 2 tablespoons (light) cream
- Red chili pepper
- Parsley

Directions

1. Finely chop the parsley and chili. Put the eggs in a bowl and stir in the cream, parsley and pepper.
2. Fill the dishes up to halfway with the egg mixture. Bake the soufflés at 200°C for 8 minutes. If you want to serve the soufflés (soft), then 5 minutes cooking is enough.

Baked Potato

Servings 6 persons, Preparation time 5 minutes, Cooking time: 25 minutes

Ingredients

- 6 potatoes
- 1 red onion or 2 spring onions
- 6-8 slices salami or chorizo
- ½ red pepper
- 100 g peas (fresh or frozen)
- 1 tbsp sour cream
- 1 tbsp fresh herbs, like chives, tarragon or parsley (optional)
- pepper & salt to taste

Directions

1. Preheat the Airfryer to 200°C.
2. Scrub the potato skins thoroughly until clean, then dry them with kitchen paper.
3. Place the potatoes in the basket of the Airfryer. Slide the basket into the Airfryer and set the timer for 25 minutes.

4. In the meantime, finely chop the onion. Cut the salami and red pepper into bite-sized pieces. Boil the peas for a few minutes until done. Rinse them under cold water, then drain and set aside.
5. When the timer rings and the potatoes are done, set them aside until they are cool enough to handle. Slice the top off each potato. Gently scoop the fluffy insides into a bowl.
6. Mash the fluffy potato insides with the sour cream using a fork. Mix in the salami, pepper, peas and the fresh herbs, if using. Season with pepper & salt. Fill the baked potatoes with the mixture and serve immediately.

Fig Tart with Goats Cheese and Honey

Servings 8 persons

Ingredients

- 7 sheets puff pastry
- 100 g goats' cheese
- Dried oregano
- Olive oil
- 200 ml Greek yogurt 0% fat
- 2 tablespoons honey
- 6 fresh figs

Directions

1. Take a loose-bottomed tin of approximately 22 cm in diameter. This fits snugly in your Airfryer (using the Grill Pan accessory). Place a sheet of parchment paper in the tin and place the puff pastry slices on top. They can hang over the edge a little.
2. Mix the Greek yogurt with the honey and salt and pepper. Spread this mixture on the puff pastry. Cut the goats' cheese into thin slices and place on top of the yogurt mixture. Sprinkle with some dried oregano.
3. Cut the figs into nice thin slices and place on the tart. Bake for 20 minutes at 170°C. Serve the tart lukewarm.

Potato Slices

Servings 4 persons, Preparation time 10 minutes, Cooking time: 26 minutes

Ingredient

- 1.2 kg large waxy potatoes
- 1 tbsp (olive) oil
- salt to taste

Directions

1. Peel the potatoes and cut each in 0.5 cm slices.
2. Soak the potatoes in water for at least 30 minutes. Drain them thoroughly, then pat them dry with kitchen paper.
3. Preheat the Airfryer to 160°C.
4. Put the potatoes in a large bowl, drizzle with the oil and toss to coat them. Transfer them to the Airfryer basket. Slide the basket into the Airfryer and set the timer for 16 minutes.
5. When the timer rings, slide out the basket and shake the potatoes. Adjust the temperature to 180°C and set the timer for another 10 minutes.

6. After 5 minutes, slide out the basket and shake the potatoes again.
7. Fry until the timer rings and the potatoes are golden brown. Sprinkle with salt and serve on a platter.

Cubed Potatoes

Servings 4 persons, Preparation time 10 minutes, Cooking time: 22 minutes

Ingredient

- 1.2 kg large waxy potatoes
- 1 tbsp (olive) oil
- salt to taste

Directions

1. Peel the potatoes and cut each into 1.5 cm cubes.
2. Soak the potatoes in water for at least 30 minutes. Drain them thoroughly, then pat them dry with kitchen paper.
3. Preheat the Airfryer to 160°C.
4. Put the potatoes in a large bowl, drizzle with the oil and toss to coat them. Transfer them to the Airfryer basket. Slide the basket into the Airfryer and set the timer for 14 minutes.

5. When the timer rings, slide out the basket and shake the potatoes. Adjust the temperature to 180°C and set the timer for another 8 minutes.
6. After 4 minutes, slide out the basket and shake the potatoes again.
7. Fry until the timer rings and the potatoes are golden brown. Sprinkle with salt and serve on a platter.

Wedged Potatoes

Servings 4 persons, Preparation time 10 minutes, Cooking time: 35 minutes

Ingredient

- 1.2 kg large waxy potatoes
- 1 tbsp (olive) oil
- salt to taste

Directions

1. Peel the potatoes and cut each in 6-8 wedges
2. Soak the potatoes in water for at least 30 minutes. Drain them thoroughly, then pat them dry with kitchen paper.
3. Preheat the Airfryer to 160°C.
4. Put the potatoes in a large bowl, drizzle with the oil and toss to coat them. Transfer them to the Airfryer basket. Slide the basket into the Airfryer and set the timer for 20 minutes.

5. When the timer rings, slide out the basket and shake the potatoes. Adjust the temperature to 180°C and set the timer for another 15 minutes.
6. After 8 minutes, slide out the basket and shake the potatoes again.
7. Fry until the timer rings and the potatoes are golden brown. Sprinkle with salt and serve on a platter.

Main Courses

Chicken Fillet with Brie and Cured Ham

Servings 4 persons, Preparation time 15 minutes, Cooking time: 15 minutes

Ingredients

- 2 large chicken fillets
- Freshly ground pepper
- 4 small slices Brie cheese
- 1 tablespoon chives, finely chopped
- 4 slices cured ham

Directions

1. Preheat the Airfryer to 180°C.
2. Cut the chicken fillets into four equal pieces and slit them horizontally to 1 cm from the edge. Open the chicken fillets and sprinkle with salt and pepper. Cover each piece with a slice of Brie and some chives.

3. Close the chicken fillets and tightly wrap a slice of ham around them. Thinly coat the stuffed fillets with olive oil and put them in the basket.
4. Slide the basket into the Airfryer and set the timer to 15 minutes. Roast the chicken fillets nicely brown and done. Delicious with mashed potatoes and stir-fried witloof chicory.
5. Replace the Brie by another cheese, such as Gouda, Cheddar or Gruyère.

Lamb Chops with Garlic Sauce

Servings 4 persons, Preparation time 15 minutes, Cooking time: 22 minutes

Ingredients

- 1 garlic bulb
- 3 tablespoons olive oil
- 1 tablespoon fresh oregano, finely chopped
- Sea salt
- Freshly ground black pepper
- 8 lamb chops

Directions

1. Preheat the Airfryer to 200°C. Thinly coat the garlic bulb with olive oil and put it in the basket. Slide the basket into the Airfryer and set the timer to 12 minutes. Roast the garlic until done.
2. In the meantime, mix the herbs with some sea salt, pepper and olive oil. Thinly coat the lamb chops with half a tablespoon of herb oil in total and leave them for 5 minutes.

3. Remove the garlic bulb from the basket and pre-heat the Airfryer to 200°C.
4. Place four lamb chops in the basket and slide the basket into the Airfryer. Set the timer to 5 minutes. Roast the lamb chops nicely brown. Inside they may still be red or pink. Keep them warm in a dish and roast the other lamb chops in the same way.
5. Squeeze the garlic cloves between thumb and index finger over the herb oil. Add some salt and pepper, and stir the mixture well.
6. Serve the lamb chops with garlic sauce. Goes well with couscous and braised zucchini.

Gambas 'Pil Pil' with Sweet Potato

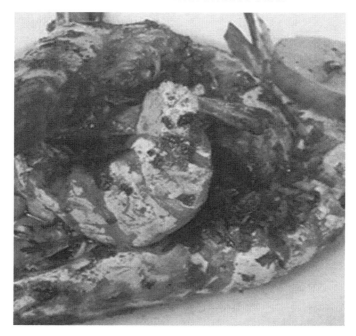

Servings 4 persons

Ingredients

- 12 King prawns
- 1 red chili pepper, de-seeded
- 1 shallot
- 4 tablespoons olive oil
- 4 stalks lemongrass
- 4 garlic cloves
- Smoked paprika powder
- 5 large sweet potatoes
- 1 tablespoon honey
- 2 tablespoons olive oil
- 2 tablespoons fresh rosemary, finely chopped
- 2 limes

Directions

1. Clean and gut the prawns. Finely slice the garlic and red chili pepper and chop up the shallots. Mix the garlic, red chili pepper, onion, and olive oil with the paprika to form a marinade and leave the prawns to marinate for 2 hours.

2. Cut the sweet potato into slices and mix with the oil, chopped rosemary and honey. Bake the potatoes for 15 minutes at 180°C in the Airfryer. Meanwhile, thread the prawns on the stalks of lemongrass. Turn the temperature to 200°C and add the prawn skewers. Cook for 5 minutes. Serve with lime wedges.

Warm Asparagus Salad

Servings 4 persons

Ingredients

- 250 g white asparagus
- 150 g green asparagus
- 2 red chicory
- 4 boiled eggs
- 250 g small pre-boiled potatoes
- 250 g ham cubes
- 6 radishes, sliced
- 2 mandarin oranges (or 1 small tin)
- 200 g cherry tomatoes, halved
- 250 g mixed salad leaves
- 1 tablespoon olive oil

Directions

1. Peel the white asparagus, cut about 1 cm off from the bottom and cut into pieces. Cut the green asparagus into pieces.

72

2. Put an ovenproof dish in your Airfryer and heat this for 5 minutes at 200°C. Once warm, add one tablespoon of olive oil, the sliced asparagus, potatoes and ham pieces. Cook this for 10 minutes at 200°C and stir occasionally.
3. Leave to cool for 5 minutes and add the mandarin, radishes, salad and tomatoes. Season the salad with salt and pepper to taste. Cut the leaves from the red chicory and the eggs into quarters. Place the chicory on a beautiful large dish and spread the salad and eggs out on it.

Turk Bread with Chicken Filling

Servings 2 persons

Ingredients

For the stuffed bread:

- 1 Turkish bread
- 500 g chicken thigh fillet, in strips
- 100 g black olives
- 200 g tomatoes
- 2 red onions
- 1 teaspoon smoked paprika powder
- 1 teaspoon cumin
- 2 tablespoons olive oil
- Pinch of chili powder
- 75 g rocket leaves

For the sauce:

- 250 g Turkish yogurt 0% fat
- 3 garlic cloves
- 15 g parsley, chopped

Directions

1. Cut the chicken into neat thin strips. Make a marinade from 2 tablespoons of olive oil, chili powder, smoked paprika powder, cumin, salt and pepper. Put the meat into the marinade, stir and leave for 1 hour.

2. Crush the garlic and cut it very finely together with the parsley. Mix with the yogurt and cover with plastic wrap. Leave this for 1 hour, so that the flavors can develop properly.

3. Heat the Airfryer to 200°C. Place the chicken in the Airfryer and cook for 10 minutes. Shake a few times. Meanwhile, cut the tomatoes into slices and the red onion into rings.

4. Cut the Turkish bread into four and fill it with the chicken, sliced tomato and onion and of course the delicious garlic sauce. Garnish with rocket.

Toad in The Hole

Servings 4 persons

Ingredients

- 1 tablespoon olive oil
- 8 small sausages
- 165 g flour
- 2 eggs
- 160 ml milk
- 120 ml cold water
- 1 clove garlic, pressed
- 1 red onion, finely sliced
- 15 g rosemary

Directions

1. Take an ovenproof dish that fits in your Airfryer and coat with oil. Sieve the flour over a medium-sized bowl and beat the eggs into it.

Gradually add the milk, water, the chopped onion and garlic and season to taste with salt and pepper. Mix everything together well.

2. Pierce and stick the sprigs of rosemary into the sausages and place in the dish. Pour the batter over the sausages.

3. Pre-heat the Airfryer to 160°C and bake the dish for 30 minutes.

Teriyaki Steak with Potatoes

Servings 2 persons

Ingredients

- 2 steaks
- 4 medium-sized potatoes
- 200 g snow peas
- 250 g mushrooms
- 1 onion
- Ketjap Manis sauce
- Soy sauce
- Olive oil
- Salt and pepper

Directions

1. Cut the steaks into strips and place them in a marinade of soy sauce, olive oil and ketjap. Brush the mushrooms clean and cut them into quarters. Wash the snow peas and cut the onion into half-rings.
2. Mix all the vegetables together with one tablespoon of olive oil.

3. Peel the potatoes and cut a small slice off the bottom so that they lie flat. Make small incisions in the potatoes, but not all the way to the bottom. Put some oil between the incisions and sprinkle the potatoes with salt and pepper.
4. Bake the potatoes in the Airfryer for 20 minutes at 190°C. Then slide the potatoes to the side and place the vegetables and the meat in the middle. Bake for 5 minutes at 200°C.

Steak Tartare Burgers with Ham

Servings 4 persons, Preparation time 10 minutes, Cooking time: 8 minutes

Ingredients

- 400 g finely minced beef
- 5 cm white of 1 leek, very finely chopped
- 50 g ham, in fine strips
- 3 tablespoons bread crumbs
- Freshly ground pepper
- Nutmeg

Directions

1. Preheat the Airfryer to 200°C. Mix the minced beef with the leek, ham, bread crumbs, some salt and pepper, and nutmeg. Knead thoroughly to obtain a homogenous mixture.
2. Divide the minced beef into four portions and form smooth burgers with wet hands.

3. Put the burgers in the basket and slide it into the Airfryer. Set the timer to 8 minutes and fry the burgers until nicely brown. Inside they may still be pink.
4. Serve the steak tartare burgers with boiled potatoes and cauliflower or broccoli.

Spicy Rolled Meat

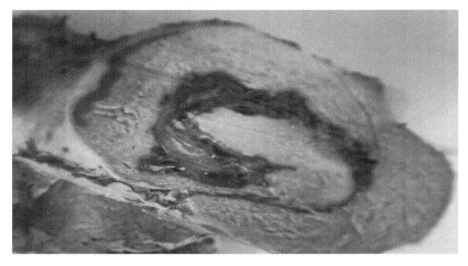

Servings 4 persons, Preparation time 15 minutes, Cooking time: 40 minutes

Ingredients

- 1 pork fricandeau or turkey breast fillet - 500 g
- 1 clove garlic, crushed
- ½ teaspoon chili powder
- 1 teaspoon cinnamon
- 1½ teaspoon ground cumin
- 2 tablespoons olive oil
- 1 small red onion, finely chopped
- 3 tablespoons flat-leafed parsley, finely chopped
- String for rolled meat

Directions

1. Place the meat on a cutting board with the short side towards you and slit it horizontally along the full length about a 1/3 of the way from the top stopping 2 cm from the edge. Fold this part open and slit it again from this side and open it. You now have a long piece of meat.

2. Mix the garlic in a bowl with the chili powder, cinnamon, cumin, pepper and 1 teaspoon salt. Add the olive oil. Spoon 1 tablespoon of this mixture in another small bowl. Mix the onion and parsley in the mixture in the big bowl.
3. Preheat the Airfryer to 180°C.
4. Coat the meat with the onion mixture. Roll the meat firmly, start at the short side. Tie the string around the meat at 3 cm intervals. Rub the outside of the rolled meat with the herb mixture.

Hot Drumsticks with Barbecue Marinade

Servings 4 persons, Preparation time 25 minutes, Cooking time: 20 minutes

Ingredients

- 1 clove garlic, crushed
- ½ tablespoon mustard
- 2 teaspoons brown sugar
- 1 teaspoon chili powder
- Freshly ground black pepper
- 1 tablespoon olive oil
- 4 drumsticks

Directions

1. Preheat the Airfryer to 200°C.
2. Mix the garlic with the mustard, brown sugar, chili powder, a pinch of salt and freshly ground pepper to taste. Mix with the oil.

3. Rub the drumsticks completely with the marinade and leave to marinate for 20 minutes.
4. Put the drumsticks in the basket and slide the basket into the Airfryer. Set the timer to 10 minutes. Roast the drumsticks until brown.
5. Then lower the temperature to 150°C and roast the drumsticks for another 10 minutes until done.
6. Serve the drumsticks with corn salad and French bread.

Souvlaki with Greek Salad and Tzatziki

Servings 4 persons

Ingredients

Souvlaki:

- 1 kg pork
- 3 teaspoons ground cumin
- 1 teaspoon paprika powder
- (Corn) oil
- Vinegar
- Greek salad:
- 1/2 cucumber
- 1 red onion
- 4 tomatoes
- 200 g feta cheese
- 50 g Greek olives
- 20 small green chili peppers (jar)
- Wine vinegar

Tzatziki:

- 2 pointed sweet peppers
- 1/2 cucumber
- Greek yogurt 0% fat
- 4 garlic cloves

Directions

1. Grate half of the cucumber and press the garlic. Mix this with the Greek yogurt and leave to infuse. Cut the meat into equal-sized cubes and make a marinade from the oil, paprika, cumin, oil, vinegar, salt and pepper. Thread the meat onto (wooden) skewers.
2. Cut the other half of the cucumber and tomato into cubes. Crumble the feta and cut the red onion into pieces. Mix the ingredients in a bowl and add the chili pepper and olives. Season to taste with vinegar, salt and pepper.
3. Halve the sweet pointed bell peppers and fill with the tzatziki. Pre-heat the Airfryer for 2 minutes at 200°C and place the Souvlaki and pointed peppers in the basket. Cook everything for 8 minutes at 200°C. Serve with the salad.

Salmon with Pesto and Roasted Tomatoes

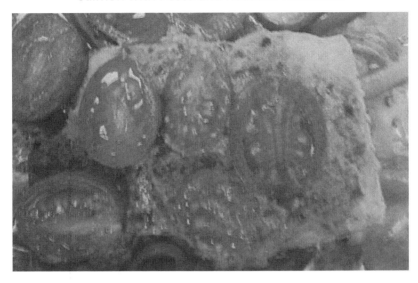

Servings 4 persons

Ingredients

- 4 salmon steaks
- 4 tablespoons pesto
- 400 g (colored) pasta
- 8 large prawns
- 250 g cherry tomatoes
- 1 lemon
- Olive oil
- Fresh thyme

Directions

1. Boil the water for the pasta and add some salt. Add the pasta when the water boils.
2. Meanwhile, take an ovenproof dish that fits in your Airfryer and coat with one tablespoon of pesto. Place the slices of salmon in the dish

and spread on the rest of the pesto. Pour on two tablespoons of olive oil. Halve the tomatoes and put them with the salmon.

3. Place the prawns on the salmon, drizzle with lemon juice and grill at 200°C for 8 minutes. Drain the pasta and serve with the salmon and prawns.

Salmon Quiche

Servings 2 persons, Preparation time 15 minutes, Cooking time: 20 minutes

Ingredients

- 150 g salmon fillet, cut into small cubes
- ½ tablespoon lemon juice
- Freshly ground black pepper
- 100 g flour
- 50 g cold butter, in cubes
- 2 eggs + 1 egg yolk
- 3 tablespoons whipping cream
- 1 green onion, sliced into 1 cm pieces

Directions

1. Preheat the Airfryer to 180°C. Mix the salmon pieces with the lemon juice and salt and pepper to taste. Allow the salmon to rest.
2. In a bowl, mix the flour with the butter, egg yolk and ½-1 tablespoon cold water and knead into a smooth ball.
3. On a floured work surface, roll out the dough to an 18 cm round.

4. Put the dough round in the quiche pan and press firmly along the edges. Trim the dough closely along the edge of the pan or allow the dough to stick out roughly over the edges of the pan.
5. Beat the eggs lightly with the cream and mustard and add salt and pepper to taste. Pour this mixture into the quiche pan and then lay the pieces of salmon in the pan. Distribute the green onion evenly over the contents of the quiche pan.
6. Place the quiche pan in the fryer basket and slide the basket into the Airfryer. Set the timer to 20 minutes and bake the quiche until golden brown and done.

Salmon and Cod Lasagna

Servings 2 persons

Ingredients

- 9 fresh lasagna sheets
- 400 g salmon
- 400 g cod fillets
- Juice of 1 lime
- 100 ml white wine
- 200 ml cream
- 200 ml milk
- 1 small broccoli
- 1 shallot
- 10 g cornstarch
- 1 tablespoon chopped parsley
- 1 tablespoon chopped chives
- Grated cheese
- Imitation caviar (optional)

Directions

1. Finely chop the broccoli, shallot, parsley and chives.
2. In a pan, bring the cream, milk, wine and cornstarch to the boil then add the chopped shallot, parsley and chives. As the sauce starts to bind, add the lime juice and season to taste with pepper, salt or some fish bouillon powder.
3. Take an oven dish that fits in the Airfryer and begin building the lasagna. Start with some sauce and a first layer of lasagna sheets. Put the sliced broccoli on the first layer and cover with another layer of lasagna sheets. Place the salmon on top, cover with a new layer and put the cod on top. Finish with a layer of sauce and grated cheese. Heat the Airfryer to 150°C and bake the lasagna for 45 minutes.
4. Spoon the lasagna onto a plate and garnish with the imitation caviar. Crisped salmon is another nice garnish. I make this by rolling up and freezing a slice of smoked salmon then grating it fine. Leave to dry in the oven on some parchment paper and you'll have a wonderful topping.

Saltimbocca - Veal Rolls with Sage

Servings 4 persons, Preparation time 15 minutes, Cooking time: 15 minutes

Ingredients

- 400 ml meat stock
- 200 ml dry white wine
- 4 veal cutlets
- Freshly ground pepper
- 8 fresh sage leaves
- 4 slices cured ham
- 25 g butter

Directions

1. Preheat the Airfryer to 200°C. Boil the meat stock and the wine in a wide pan on medium heat until it has reduced to one-third of the original amount.
2. Sprinkle salt and pepper on the cutlets and cover them with the sage leaves. Firmly roll the cutlets and wrap a slice of ham around each cutlet.

3. Thinly brush the entire cutlets with butter and place them in the basket. Slide the basket into the Airfryer and set the timer to 10 minutes. Roast the veal rolls until nicely brown.
4. Lower the temperature to 150°C and set the timer to 5 minutes. Roast the rolls until done. Mix the remainder of the butter with the reduced stock and season the gravy with salt and pepper.
5. Thinly slice the veal rolls and serve them with the gravy.

Roasted Rack of Lamb with a Macadamia Crust

Servings 4 persons, Preparation time 10 minutes, Cooking time: 30 minutes

Ingredients

- 1 garlic clove
- 1 tbsp olive oil
- 800 g rack of lamb
- pepper & salt
- 75 g unsalted macadamia nuts
- 1 tbsp breadcrumbs (preferably homemade)
- 1 tbsp chopped fresh rosemary
- 1 egg

Directions

1. Finely chop the garlic. Mix the olive oil and garlic to make garlic oil. Brush the rack of lamb with the oil and season with pepper & salt.
2. Preheat the Airfryer to 100°C.
3. Finely chop the nuts and place them into a bowl. Stir in the breadcrumbs and rosemary. Whisk the egg in another bowl.
4. To coat the lamb, dip the meat into the egg mixture, draining off any excess. Coat the lamb with the macadamia crust.
5. Put the coated lamb rack in the Airfryer basket and slide the basket into the Airfryer. Set the timer for 25 minutes. After 25 minutes, increase the temperature to 200°C and set the timer for another 5 minutes. Remove the meat and leave to rest, covered with aluminium foil, for 10 minutes before serving.
6. You can replace the macadamia nuts with pistachios, hazelnuts, cashews or almonds if desired.

Roasted Vegetables

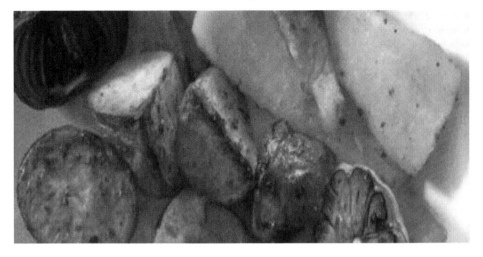

Servings 6 persons, Preparation time 5 minutes, Cooking time: 20 minutes

Ingredients

- 300 g parsnips
- 300 g celeriac
- 2 red onions
- 300 g 'butternut squash'
- 1 tbsp fresh thyme needles
- 1 tbsp olive oil
- pepper & salt

Directions

1. Preheat the Airfryer to 200°C.
2. Peel the parsnips, celeriac and onions. Cut the parsnips and celeriac into 2 cm cubes and the onions into wedges. Halve the 'butternut squash', remove the seeds and cut into cubes. (Not necessary to peel it.)
3. Mix the cut vegetables with the thyme and olive oil. Season to taste.

4. Place the vegetables into the basket and slide the basket into the Airfryer. Set the timer for 20 minutes and roast the vegetables until the timer rings and the vegetables are nicely brown and done. Stir the vegetables once while roasting.

Ratatouille

Servings 4 persons, Preparation time 8 minutes, Cooking time: 15 minutes

Ingredients

- 200 g courgette and/or aubergine
- 1 yellow bell pepper
- 2 tomatoes
- 1 onion, peeled
- 1 clove garlic, crushed
- 2 teaspoons dried Provençal herbs
- Freshly ground black pepper
- 1 tablespoon olive oil
- Small, round baking dish, 16 cm diameter

Directions

1. Preheat the Airfryer to 200°C.
2. Cut the courgette, aubergine, bell pepper, tomatoes, and onion into 2 cm cubes.

3. Mix the vegetables in a bowl with the garlic, Provençal herbs, ½ teaspoon salt and pepper to taste. Also spoon in the olive oil.
4. Put the bowl in the basket and slide the basket into the Airfryer. Set the timer to 15 minutes and cook the ratatouille. Stir the vegetables once when cooking.
5. Serve the ratatouille with fried meat.

Rack of Lamb

Servings 4 persons

Ingredients

- 2 racks of lamb
- 1 bunch fresh mint
- 2 garlic cloves
- 100 ml extra virgin olive oil
- 1 tablespoon honey
- Freshly ground pepper
- Kitchen twine

Directions

1. Put the mint, garlic, oil and honey in the chopper of a hand blender. Puree the ingredients into a nice thin mint pesto.

2. Make a small incision in the lamb racks, from the top between the bones, then tie the rack into a kind of crown shape using kitchen twine. Smear generously with the pesto. Keep a little of the pesto to one side.

3. Heat the Airfryer to 200°C and place the grill pan accessory in it. Cook the lamb rack for 15 minutes at 200 degrees. Open the Airfryer every 5 minutes to smear the crown with another layer of pesto.

4. Serve with mashed potatoes and fresh vegetables.

Quiche Lorraine

Servings 8 persons

Ingredients

- 250 g fine wheat flour
- 100 g butter
- 5 g yeast (dried)
- 5 g salt
- 5 g (super-fine) sugar
- 100 ml milk
- 1 egg
- 250 g lean bacon
- 250 g lean ham cubes
- 100 g mushrooms
- 100 g onion
- 300 g grated cheese
- 3 eggs
- 300 ml cream
- Salt and pepper
- Chives, finely chopped

Directions

1. Mix the eggs, cream and chives with some salt and pepper and put it in the refrigerator.
2. Put the yeast with the sugar in a bowl and mix with lukewarm milk. Let the mixture rest for a while and, in the meantime, sift the flour. Sprinkle the flour in a bowl or on your worktop and make a well in the middle. Add the egg, butter and the yeast mixture. Knead the dough from the inside out. Gradually add more and more flour to the wet mixture. Knead the dough well.
3. Grease a bowl with a small amount of oil and place the dough in it to rise. The oil ensures that the dough does not stick to the bowl. Leave a damp cloth over the bowl and let the dough rise for one hour.
4. Cut the bacon and ham into cubes, clean the mushrooms and cut them into thin slices. Finely dice the onion.
5. If you have a regular sized Airfryer, divide your dough into four equal pieces. Grease the spring forms with a little oil or butter and place a sheet of parchment paper on top. Roll out the dough and put it in the tin. Prick a few holes in the dough to prevent air bubbles from forming.
6. Fill the tin(s) with the onion, bacon, ham, mushrooms and cheese. Then add the egg mixture and fold the excess dough on the edges to the inside. Place the spring form tin in the Airfryer and bake the quiche(s).
7. Cooking times: regular sized Airfryer: 30 minutes at 160°C (per quiche) Airfryer XL: 40 minutes at 150°C.
8. Regular Airfryer preparation: 4 16 cm spring form tins. Airfryer XL preparation: 1 20 cm spring form tin.

Potatoes au Gratin

Servings 4 persons, Preparation time 10 minutes, Cooking time: 15 minutes

Ingredients

- 400 g slightly starchy potatoes, peeled
- 50 ml milk
- 50 ml cream
- Freshly ground pepper
- Nutmeg
- 40 g Gruyère or semi-mature cheese, grated

Directions

1. Preheat the Airfryer to 200°C. Slice the potatoes wafer-thin.
2. In a bowl, mix the milk and the cream and season to taste with salt, pepper and nutmeg. Coat the potato slices with the milk mixture.
3. Transfer the potato slices to the quiche pan and pour the rest of the cream mixture from the bowl on top of the potatoes. Distribute the cheese evenly over the potatoes.

4. Place the quiche pan in the fryer basket and slide the basket into the Airfryer. Set the timer to 15 minutes and bake the gratin until it is nicely browned and done.
5. Serve the potatoes au gratin in squares with fish or roasts

Paella à la Martin

Servings 4 persons

Ingredients

- 150 g paella rice
- 50 g peas
- 50 g red bell pepper
- 400 ml dry white wine
- 100 ml water
- 2 sachets paella herbs
- 50 g squid, in pieces
- 200 g mussels
- 100 g sea bass fillet
- 100 g clams
- 6 scallops
- 4 large prawns
- 4 crayfish
- Olive oil
- 1 lemon

Directions

1. Take an ovenproof dish and heat for 10 minutes at 200°C. Cut the sea bass fillet into pieces and wash the mussels and clams. Pour a glug of olive oil in the warm dish and add the sea bass, prawns, mussels, clams, squid and scallops. Turn a few times.
2. Mix the peas, sliced bell pepper, paella herbs and one teaspoon of salt with the uncooked rice and place it on the fish. Add the white wine and water to cover the rice. Cook for 30 minutes at 200°C and stir the rice occasionally. Make sure that the shells and the fish stay beneath the rice.
3. Serve the paella with the crayfish and lemon.

Pizza with Salami, Mozzarella and Olives

Servings 2 persons

Ingredients

- 200 g 00-flour
- 100 g water
- 1 sachet dried yeast
- 2 tablespoons olive oil
- 10 g salt
- 5 g sugar
- Tomato sauce
- 8 salami slices
- 12 mozzarella balls
- 10 small cherry tomatoes
- 10 black olives
- 1 red chili pepper, de-seeded
- 1 yellow bell pepper
- Fresh basil
- Dried oregano

Directions

1. Start by making a yeast dough: mix the yeast with the lukewarm water. Sift the flour, place it on your worktop and make a well in the center. Sprinkle the salt and the sugar on the edge. Pour the oil and the yeast mixture in the well and work carefully from the inside out. Knead to an elastic dough. If you have a food processor with dough hook, let it do the hard work and put it on setting 3. Divide the dough into two pieces and let it rise for a minimum of one hour under a damp cloth.

2. Cut the cherry tomatoes in half. Remove the seeds from the pepper and cut into small pieces. Cut the olives into rings and the bell peppers into strips. After one hour, roll the dough onto the grill pan accessory (approximately 1/2 cm bigger than your grill pan) and spread the dough with the tomato sauce. Put all ingredients on the tomato sauce and bake the pizza for 8-10 minutes at 180°C. Sprinkle with the basil.

Pizza with Salami and Mushrooms

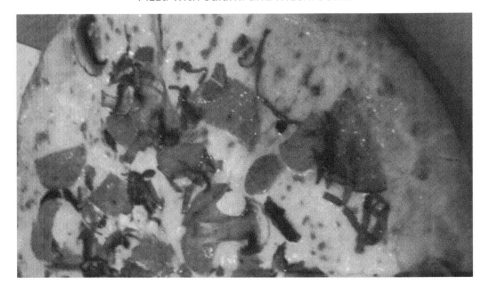

Servings 1 persons, Preparation time 15 minutes, Cooking time: 12 minutes

Ingredients

- 100 g flour
- 1 teaspoon instant yeast
- ½ tablespoon olive oil
- 50 ml tomato sauce
- ½ ball of mozzarella, sliced thinly
- 50 g salami, in strips
- 2-3 mushrooms, sliced
- 2 teaspoons dried oregano
- Freshly ground black pepper
- 2 tablespoons Parmesan cheese, grated
- Handful of arugula
- Small pizza pan, 15 cm diameter, buttered

Directions

1. Mix the flour with the yeast, a pinch of salt, olive oil and 60-75 ml water into a smooth dough ball. Knead this dough ball until it becomes flexible and elastic.
2. Preheat the Airfryer to 200°C.
3. On a floured work surface, roll out the dough to an 18 cm round and put this dough round in the pizza pan. Fold the excess edge of the dough inward to form a crust.
4. Evenly spread the tomato sauce over the dough and place the mozzarella slices on top. Distribute the salami and mushrooms over the cheese. Sprinkle the pizza with oregano, pepper and Parmesan cheese.
5. Place the pizza pan in the fryer basket and slide the basket into the Airfryer. Set the timer to 12 minutes and bake the pizza until golden brown.
6. Your pizza will be ready faster if you use ready-to-use pizza dough.

Pork Satay with Peanut Sauce

Servings 4 persons, Preparation time 35 minutes, Cooking time: 10 minutes

Ingredients

- 2 cloves garlic, crushed
- 2 cm fresh ginger root, grated or 1 teaspoon ginger powder
- 2 teaspoons chili paste or hot pepper sauce
- 2-3 tablespoons sweet soy sauce
- 2 tablespoons vegetable oil
- 400 g lean pork chops, in cubes of 3 cm
- 1 shallot, finely chopped
- 1 teaspoon ground coriander
- 200 ml coconut milk
- 100 g unsalted

Directions

1. Mix half of the garlic in a dish with the ginger, 1 teaspoon hot pepper sauce, 1 tablespoon soy sauce, and 1 tablespoon oil. Mix the meat with the mixture and leave to marinate for 15 minutes.
2. Preheat the Airfryer to 200°C.
3. Put the marinated meat in the basket and slide it into the Airfryer. Set the timer to 12 minutes and roast the meat until brown and done. Turn once while roasting.
4. In the meantime, make the peanut sauce: heat 1 tablespoon oil in a saucepan and gently sauté the shallot with the remainder of the garlic. Add the coriander and fry for a short time more.
5. Mix the coconut milk and the peanuts with 1 teaspoon hot pepper sauce and 1 tablespoon soy sauce with the shallot mixture and gently boil for 5 minutes, while stirring. If necessary, add a little bit of water if the sauce gets too thick. Season to taste with soy sauce and hot pepper sauce.

Mediterranean Chicken Nuggets

Servings 4 persons, Preparation time 20 minutes, Cooking time: 20 minutes

Ingredients

- 2 slices stale white bread, in pieces
- 1 tablespoon (spicy) paprika powder
- 250 g chicken fillet, in pieces
- 1 egg yolk + 2 egg whites
- 1 clove garlic, crushed
- 2 tablespoons red pesto
- Freshly ground pepper

Directions

1. Grind the bread with the paprika powder in the food processor until you have a crumbly mixture and mix in the olive oil. Transfer this mixture to a bowl.
2. Then purée the chicken fillet in the food processor and mix with the egg yolk, garlic, pesto, and parsley. Add ½ teaspoon salt and pepper to taste.
3. Preheat the Airfryer to 200°C.
4. Whisk the egg whites in a bowl. Shape the chicken mixture into 10 balls and press them into oval nuggets. Coat the nuggets first with egg white and then with breadcrumbs. The nuggets must be coated with crumbs all over.
5. Put five nuggets in the basket and slide it into the Airfryer. Set the timer to 10 minutes. Fry the nuggets golden brown. Then fry the remainder of the nuggets. Can serve with French fries and a fresh salad.

Noodles with Chicken, Glasswort and Shiitake Mushrooms

Servings 4 persons

Ingredients

- 400 g Udon noodles
- 400 g chicken thigh fillets
- 4 tablespoons soy sauce
- 1 tablespoon sesame seeds
- 1 teaspoon sambal
- 1 red onion
- 2 garlic cloves
- 2 tablespoons sesame oil
- 150 g Shiitake mushrooms
- 150 g chestnut mushrooms
- 200 g glasswort
- 150 g bean sprouts
- Krupuk

Directions

1. Cut the chicken into pieces and make a marinade of soy sauce, sambal and garlic. Mix the marinade with the chicken and leave to infuse.
2. Prepare the noodles according to the packaging and drain. Then mix with one tablespoon of sesame oil.
3. Heat the Airfryer to 200°C. Cook the chicken for 6 minutes at 200°C and give it a good few shakes. Add the mushrooms, onion, bean sprouts and glasswort and cook for 5 minutes. Add the noodles, cook these together with the vegetables and chicken for another 5 minutes. Add the krupuk with one minute left to go.
4. Sprinkle the wok dish with sesame seeds.

Bratwurst Special

Servings 4 persons

Ingredients

- 400 g flour, sifted
- Dried yeast
- 2 teaspoons salt
- 4 tablespoons sugar
- 20 g baking powder
- 1 egg yolk, whisked
- Coarse sea salt
- 4 brown crusty bread rolls
- 4 Bratwurst
- Mustard
- Sauerkraut

Directions

1. Make a nice dough from the flour, yeast, 2 teaspoons of salt, sugar, baking powder and 200 ml of warm water. If you have a food processor, you can let this do the heavy work. Divide the dough into four equal pieces and shape it into balls. Leave the dough balls to rest for 10 minutes then roll them out into strands in three stages. Leave a break of 10 minutes between each stage. The strands should be the thickness of a pencil.

2. Make a pretzel shape with the strands and boil them in a pan with water and 3 tablespoons of baking powder for one minute. Sprinkle the pretzels with coarse sea salt. Heat your Airfryer to 180°C and bake the pretzels for 10 minutes until nice and brown and crispy. It's best to use the grill pan accessory. Pre-cooking them in water with baking powder will let the pretzels break open. Then bake the bread rolls and bratwursts at 200°C for 8 minutes.

Pork Tenderloin with Bell Pepper

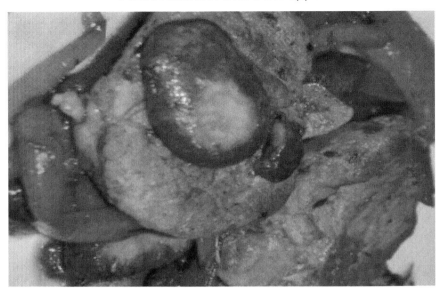

Servings 2 persons, Preparation time 10 minutes, Cooking time: 15 minutes

Ingredients

- 1 red or yellow bell pepper, in thin strips
- 1 red onion, in thin slices
- 2 teaspoons Provençal herbs
- Freshly ground black pepper
- 1 tablespoon olive oil
- 1 pork tenderloin - 300 g
- ½ tablespoon mustard
- Round 15 cm oven dish

Directions

1. Preheat the Airfryer to 200°C.
2. In the dish, mix the bell pepper strips with the onion, the Provençal herbs, and some salt and pepper to taste. Add ½ tablespoon olive oil to the mixture.

3. Cut the pork tenderloin into four pieces and rub with salt, pepper and mustard. Thinly coat the pieces with olive oil and place them upright in the dish on top of the pepper mixture.
4. Place the bowl in the basket and slide the basket into the Airfryer. Set the timer to 15 minutes and roast the meat and the vegetables.
5. Turn the meat and mix the peppers halfway through the preparation time. Great with mashed potatoes and a fresh salad.

Honey & Lime Chicken Stuffed with Zucchini

Servings 4 persons

Ingredients

- 1 whole chicken

For the filling:

- 2 tablespoons olive oil
- 2 red onions
- 1 green zucchini
- 1 yellow zucchini
- 1 sweet apple
- 2 apricots
- Fresh thyme

For the marinade:

- 200 g honey
- Juice of 1 large lemon
- Freshly ground pepper
- Salt

Directions

1. Chop all the ingredients for the filling into small cubes and mix with the oil in a bowl. Season to taste with salt and pepper. Fill the chicken with the mixture.
2. Heat the Airfryer to 200 °C. If you have the grill pan accessory you can use this to place the chicken on, so you have more space in your Airfryer. The regular sized models fit a chicken of up to 1.2 kg; the XL models usually up to 1.6 kg. Place the chicken in the Airfryer and sear the meat for 5 minutes.
3. Meanwhile, melt the honey in a pan with the juice of the lemon and season it to taste with salt and pepper. Take the chicken out of the Airfryer and cover it in some of the marinade. Set the temperature of the Airfryer to 150°C and put the chicken back in. Open the Airfryer every 15 minutes to cover the chicken with marinade until it has all gone. After 60 minutes, the chicken will be cooked. There are two ways to check whether the chicken is cooked. Either with a meat thermometer (temperature must be 85°C) or by checking the color of the liquid. When cooked, the liquid will run clear and show no pink.

Leg of Lamb with Brussels Sprouts and Potato Quenelles

Servings 4 persons

Ingredients

For the leg of lamb:

- 1 kg leg of lamb
- 2 spoons groundnut oil
- 15 g rosemary
- 15 g lemon thyme
- 1 garlic clove
- 600 g Brussels sprouts
- **For the quenelles:**
- 4 large potatoes
- A knob of butter
- Nutmeg
- No milk

Directions

1. Take a nice leg of lamb, score and stud with a few large sprigs of rosemary and lemon thyme. Smear the leg with the groundnut oil. Heat the Airfryer to 150°C and cook the lamb for 75 minutes.
2. Potato quenelles are simple to make and, as I previously mentioned, can be prepared in advance and frozen. Mash the potatoes and season to taste adding milk, butter and nutmeg. Form the quenelles using two spoons, transferring the mash from one spoon to the other. If you choose to make the quenelles in advance, they need to cook for 15 minutes at 200°C. If you prepared them fresh, they only need 8 minutes.
3. Clean and tail the Brussels sprouts and mix with some honey and neutral oil. After 75 minutes cooking time, add the sprouts and the frozen quenelles to the Airfryer. Bake the lamb, sprouts and quenelles together for 15 minutes at 200°C. If you prepared the quenelles from fresh, just add them 7 minutes after the Brussels sprouts.

Meat Loaf

Servings 4 persons, Preparation time 10 minutes, Cooking time: 25 minutes

Ingredients

- 400 g (lean) ground beef
- 1 egg, lightly beaten
- 3 tablespoons bread crumbs
- 50 g salami or chorizo sausage, finely chopped
- 1 small onion, finely chopped
- 1 tablespoon (fresh) thyme
- Freshly ground pepper
- 2 mushrooms, thick slices

Directions

1. Preheat the Airfryer to 200°C.
2. Mix the ground meat in a bowl with the egg, bread crumbs, salami, onion, thyme, 1 teaspoon salt and a generous amount of pepper. Knead and mix thoroughly.

3. Transfer the ground meat to the pan or dish and smoothen the top. Press in the mushrooms and coat the top with olive oil.
4. Place the pan or dish in the basket and slide the basket into the Airfryer. Set the timer to 25 minutes and roast the meat loaf until nicely brown and done.
5. Leave the meat loaf to stand for at least 10 minutes before serving. Then cut the loaf into wedges. Possible to serve with fried potatoes and a salad.

Grilled Vegetables with Lamb

Servings 2 persons

Ingredients

- 4 lamb chops
- ½ bunch fresh mint
- 3 tablespoons olive oil
- 1 parsnip
- 1 yellow carrot
- 1 fennel bulb
- 1 purple carrot
- Salt and pepper
- Fresh rosemary

Directions

1. Chop the mint and rosemary very finely or use a hand blender or mincer. Add 4 tablespoons of olive oil and season the marinade to taste with salt and pepper. Marinate the lamb chops for at least 3

130

hours. Cut the vegetables into small cubes and leave them to soak in a container of water. Heat your Airfryer to 200°C and sear the lamb chops for 2 minutes. Remove the chops from the basket and cover the bottom with the (drained) vegetables. Place the lamb chops on top. Cook for another 6 minutes at 200°C. Goes well with mashed potatoes with rosemary.

Grilled Fish Fillet with Pesto Sauce

Servings 3 persons, Preparation time 10 minutes, Cooking time: 8 minutes

Ingredients

- 3 white fish fillets (200 g each)
- 1 tbsp olive oil
- pepper & salt
- 1 bunch fresh basil (15 g)
- 2 garlic cloves
- 2 tbsp pinenuts
- 1 tbsp grated parmesan cheese
- 250 ml extra virgin olive oil

Directions

2. Preheat the Airfryer to 180°C.
3. Brush the fish fillets with the oil and season with pepper & salt. Place in the cooking basket of the Airfryer and slide the basket into the Airfryer. Set the timer for 8 minutes.
4. Pick the basil leaves and place them with the garlic, pinenuts, parmesan cheese and olive oil in a food processor or pestle and

132

mortar. Pulse or grind the mixture until it turns into a sauce. Add some salt to taste.

5. Place the fish fillets on a serving plate and serve them drizzled with the pesto sauce.

6. To vary, you can cover the fish in pesto sauce and cover with breadcrumbs before cooking it in the Airfryer.

Grilled Stuffed Lobster

Servings 2 persons

Ingredients

- 1 lobster
- 15 g basil
- 1 zucchini
- 1 lemon
- 30 g butter
- Olive oil

Directions

1. Cook the lobster for 5 minutes until nice and red. If you are using frozen lobster, let it defrost first. If you're using a live lobster, do as follows: a live lobster must certainly not suffer unnecessarily, so make sure the water is completely boiling. Immerse it in the water, with the head first so that it dies instantly.

2. The lobster is cooked when it is completely red. Remove the lobster from the pan with a skimmer and let it cool. Place the lobster on a chopping board and pick up a large, sharp knife. Place the point of

the knife in the groove between the eyes of the lobster. Cut the lobster in half. Then remove the intestinal tract, liver and stomach.
3. Cut the zucchini in long slices and coat them with a little olive oil. Tear the basil leaves from the sprigs and keep 10 leaves aside. Finely chop the remaining leaves and mix with the soft butter. Season the butter with salt and pepper to taste.
4. Place the lobster halves with the open side on top on the grill pan and coat with the butter. Grill the lobster at 180°C for 8 to 10 minutes. Remove the lobster from the grill pan and let it rest for a while in foil.
5. Grill the zucchini slices for 4 to 5 minutes at 200°C. Place the lobster and the zucchini slices in a dish and sprinkle with a little lemon juice. Garnish the lobster with lemon segments and the remaining basil leaves.

Grilled Pork Tenderloin with Potatoes and Green Beans

Servings 2 persons

Ingredients

- 2 pork tenderloins
- 4 potatoes (mealy)
- 400 green beans (frozen)
- 6 slices bacon
- 1 tablespoon oil

Directions

1. Preheat the Airfryer to 200°C. Clean the potatoes, score a little cross with a small knife and put them in the Airfryer. Part-bake the potatoes for 15 minutes.
2. Meanwhile, prepare the green beans wrapped in bacon. Coat the pork tenderloin with some neutral oil, such as sunflower or Canola oil. Once the potatoes have been cooking for 15 minutes, add your pork tenderloin and cook for 5 minutes more. Remove the meat after

5 minutes, place the bean/bacon rolls in the basket and place the pork tenderloin back in, on top. Cook for another 7 minutes.

3. If you don't like the skin of the potato, carefully remove it. Good with a creamy pepper sauce.

Fish and Chips

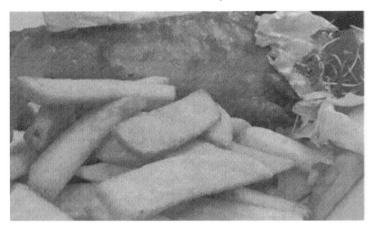

Servings 2 persons, Preparation time 15 minutes, Cooking time: 12 minutes

Ingredients

- 200 g white fish filet (tilapia, cod, pollack)
- 30 g tortilla chips
- 1 egg
- 300 g (red) potatoes
- 1 tablespoon vegetable oil
- ½ tablespoon lemon juice

Directions

1. Preheat the Airfryer to 180°C.
2. Cut the fish into four equal pieces and rub with lemon juice, salt, and pepper. Let the fish rest for 5 minutes.
3. Grind the tortilla chips very fine in the food processor and transfer the ground tortilla chips to a plate. Beat the egg in a deep dish.
4. Dip the pieces of fish into the egg one by one and roll the pieces of fish through the ground tortilla chips so that they are completely covered.
5. Scrub the potatoes clean and cut them lengthwise into thin strips. Soak the potato strips in water for at least 30 minutes. Drain them

thoroughly and then pat them dry with kitchen paper. Coat them with oil in a boil.

6. Insert the separator in the Airfryer basket. Position the potato strips on one side and the pieces of fish on the other.

7. Slide the basket into the Airfryer. Set the timer to 12 minutes and fry the potatoes and the fish until they are crispy brown.

Fried Meatballs in Tomato Sauce

Servings 3 persons, Preparation time 10 minutes, Cooking time: 8 minutes

Ingredients

- 1 small onion
- 300 g minced beef
- 1 tbsp chopped fresh parsley
- ½ tbsp chopped fresh thyme leaves
- 1 egg
- 3 tbsp breadcrumbs
- pepper & salt to taste
- 200 ml of your favourite tomato sauce

Directions

1. Finely chop the onion. Place all the ingredients into a bowl and mix well. Shape the mixture into 10 to 12 balls.
2. Preheat the Airfryer to 200°C.
3. Place the meatballs in the Airfryer basket and slide the basket in the Airfryer. Set the timer for 7 minutes.
4. Transfer the meatballs to an oven dish, add the tomato sauce and place the dish into the basket of the Airfryer. Slide the basket into the

Airfryer. Turn the temperature to 160°C and set the timer for 5 minutes to warm everything through.

5. For a great snack, you can serve the meatballs without the tomato sauce.

Special XXL Burger

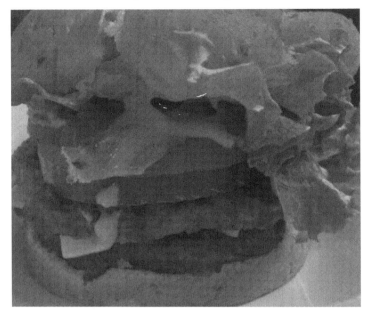

Servings 1 persons

Ingredients

- 2 burgers (beef)
- 2 burger buns
- 1 tomato
- 1 red onion
- 2 slices cheddar cheese
- Mayonnaise
- Ketchup
- Garden cress
- Lollo rosso lettuce

Directions

1. Pre-heat the Airfryer when you are cooking meat. Then place the burgers in the Airfryer and cook them for 5 minutes at 200°C.

Cut the bread buns through the center. You only need two bottom halves and a top half.

2. Squirt some ketchup on one bottom and some mayonnaise on the other. Wash the lettuce, cut the tomato into slices and the onion into thin rings. Place the lettuce, tomato and onion on the bottoms. Open the Airfryer, place the cheddar cheese on the burgers and cook for 2 minutes at 200°C.

3. Put the hamburger together and reinforce it with a cocktail stick.

Drunken Ham with Mustard

Servings 4 persons

Ingredients

- 1 joint of ham, approximately 750 g
- 2 tablespoons honey
- 2 tablespoons French mustard
- 200 ml whiskey

Directions

1. Remove the ham from the refrigerator half an hour before cooking to bring to room temperature. Take a casserole dish that fits in the Airfryer and make the marinade. For the marinade, mix the whiskey honey and mustard.
2. Place the ham in the oven dish and turn it in the marinade. Heat the Airfryer to 160°C and cook the ham for 15 minutes.
3. Add another shot of whiskey and turn in the marinade again. Cook the ham for 25 minutes until done at 160°C.
4. Great with potatoes and fresh vegetables from the Airfryer.

Courgette Stuffed with Ground Meat

Servings persons, Preparation time 20 minutes, Cooking time: 20 minutes

Ingredients

- 1 large courgette (approx. 400 g)
- 50 g feta cheese, crumbled
- 1 clove garlic, crushed
- ½ tablespoon mild paprika powder
- 200 g lean ground beef
- Freshly ground black pepper
- Shallow bowl, diameter 15 cm

Directions

1. Cut the ends off the courgette and cut it into six equal parts. Set the parts upright and carve them out with a teaspoon to 1/2 cm off the sides and 1 cm off the bottom. Sprinkle the inside with a little salt.
2. Preheat the Airfryer to 180°C.
3. Mix the ground beef with the feta cheese, garlic, paprika powder and pepper to taste and mix well. Divide the ground beef into six equal portions. Fill the hollow courgette parts with ground beef and press in the mixture. Smooth the top with a moist hand.
4. Put the courgette in the bowl and place the bowl in the basket. Slide the basket into the Airfryer and set the timer to 20 minutes. Bake the stuffed courgette until it is brown and done. Delicious with yellow rice and roasted cherry tomatoes.

Desserts and Baked Treats

Tarte Tatin

Servings 2 persons, Preparation time 15 minutes, Cooking time: 25 minutes

Ingredients

- 60 g cold butter, in thin slices
- 1 egg yolk
- 100 g flour
- 1 large, firm apple (Elstar, Jonagold)
- 30 g sugar
- Small, round fixed-base cake pan, 15 cm diameter

Directions

1. Cut 25 g of the butter slices into pieces and mix them into the flour with the egg yolk. Add a few drops of water, if necessary, and knead the mixture until it forms a smooth ball of dough.
2. On a floured work surface, roll out the dough to a 15 cm round.
3. Preheat the Airfryer to 200°C.
4. Peel and core the apple and slice the fruit into 12 wedges.
5. Place the remaining butter slices in the pan and sprinkle the sugar over them. Place the apple wedges on top of this in a circular pattern.
6. Cover the apple wedges with the rolled-out dough and press the dough down along the inside edge of the cake pan.
7. Put the cake pan in the fryer basket and slide the basket into the Airfryer. Set the timer to 25 minutes and bake until the tarte tatin is done. Immediately after baking, place a plate on the cake pan and flip the cake pan and the plate together so that the tart drops out onto the plate. Serve the tarte tatin hot or lukewarm in slices with ice cream or vanilla sauce.

Ricotta and Lemon Cheesecake

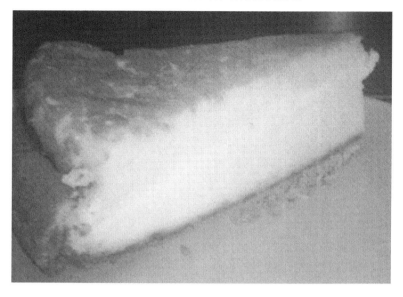

Servings 8 persons, Preparation time 10 minutes, Cooking time: 25 minutes

Ingredients

- 1 (organic) lemon
- 500 g ricotta
- 150 g sugar
- 2 tsp vanilla essence
- 3 eggs
- 3 tbsp corn starch
- 20 cm round oven dish

Directions

1. Preheat the Airfryer to 160°C.
2. Zest and juice the lemon. In a bowl, combine the ricotta, sugar, vanilla essence, 1 tbsp lemon juice and the lemon zest. Stir the ingredients until they are well combined and form a homogenous consistency.

3. Add the eggs one at a time and stir well. Add the corn starch and mix well. Pour the mixture into the oven dish.
4. Place the dish into the Airfryer basket and slide the basket into the Airfryer. Set the timer for 25 minutes. The cheesecake is ready when the timer rings and the centre is set. Place the dish on a wire rack and leave to cool completely.

Stuffed Baked Apples

Servings 2 persons, Preparation time 10 minutes, Cooking time: 20 minutes

Ingredient

- 2 small apples
- 1 tablespoon raisins
- 2 sheets of ready-to-use puff pastry, 10 x 10 cm

Directions

1. Preheat the Airfryer to 180°C.
2. Peel and core the apples. Enlarge the hollowed-out core a little by scooping out some extra apple.
3. Mix the raisins and the jam.
4. Place an apple on each slice of dough and fill the hollowed-out core with the raisin mixture. Fold the dough around the apple, enclosing it completely.
5. Place the stuffed apples on the pizza pan with the dough seams facing downward. Then brush the dough with milk.

6. Put the pizza pan in the fryer basket and slide the basket into the Airfryer. Set the timer to 20 minutes and bake the stuffed apples until golden brown and done.
7. Allow the stuffed baked apples to cool until they are lukewarm and serve them with a scoop of ice cream or vanilla quark (curd cheese).
8. Variations: Fill the apples with: -Chopped dried apricots, cinnamon and ½ tablespoon soft brown sugar - Dried cranberries, 1 teaspoon scrapings of vanilla pod and ½ tablespoon sugar -Raisins, ½ tablespoon grated orange peel and ½ tablespoon brown sugar

Red Berry Pavlova

Servings 4 persons

Ingredient

- 1 lemon, washed
- 5 eggs, separated
- 100 g super-fine sugar
- 2 teaspoons cornstarch, sieved
- 50 g strawberries
- 50 g raspberries
- 50 g black grapes
- 25 g blueberries
- 1 teaspoon lemon juice
- ½ tablespoon powdered sugar
- 200 ml whipped cream
- Red food coloring

Directions

1. Heat the Airfryer to 160°C. Grate the zest of the lemon - only the skin, the pith is very bitter - and squeeze the fruit.
2. Beat the egg whites until stiff in a dry, clean bowl. Gradually add the super-fine sugar, corn starch, lemon juice and coloring. The egg whites are ready when they become shiny and form peaks.
3. Cut a piece of parchment paper to size and place on the grill pan accessory. Smooth the paper with the mixture to create a lovely pattern. Place the pan in the Airfryer, set the temperature to 100°C and bake for 45 minutes. We preheat the Airfryer at a higher temperature so that it is nice and hot when the meringue goes in, stopping it from running.
4. Switch off the Airfryer after the cooking time, but leave it shut. Leave the meringue in the warm Airfryer for 60 minutes. Then remove from the Airfryer and leave to cool.
5. Meanwhile, mix the fruit, keeping a little behind for garnish, and whip the cream until stiff. Once the meringue has cooled, carefully cut it horizontally through the center. Pipe or spread the whipped cream on the bottom layer and fill with the fruit. Place the other half on top and garnish with the rest of the fruit.

Pineapple with Honey and Coconut

Servings 4 persons, Preparation time 10 minutes, Cooking time: 10 minutes

Ingredients

- ½ small fresh pineapple
- 1 tablespoon honey
- ½ tablespoon lime juice
- ¼ liter ice cream or mango sorbet
- Parchment paper

Directions

1. Preheat the Airfryer to 200°C. Line the bottom of the basket with baking parchment, leave 1 cm of the edge open.
2. Cut the pineapple lengthways into eight sections. Cut away the skin with the deep crowns and also remove the tough core.

155

3. Mix the honey with the lime juice in a bowl. Brush the pineapple sections with the honey and put them in the basket. Sprinkle the coconut on top.
4. Slide the basket into the Airfryer and set the timer to 12 minutes. The pineapple with the coconut should be hot and golden brown.
5. Serve the pineapple sections on plates, each with a generous scoop of ice cream next to it.
6. TIP: Spicy Pineapple - Mix 1 finely chopped red chili or 1 teaspoon of red chili paste through the honey mixture, together with 1 tablespoon finely chopped, fresh coriander. - Prepare the pineapple sections according to the recipe. These spicy pineapple sections are nice as a side dish for Asian food, but also delicious as a dessert. For dessert, serve the pineapple with coconut ice cream.

Layered Strawberry Cake

Servings 8 persons

Ingredients

For the sponge:

- 150 g sugar
- 150 g flour, sifted
- 5 eggs
- Pinch of salt
- Cream:
- 700 ml whole milk
- 1 vanilla pod
- 7 egg yolks
- 100 g powdered sugar
- 80 g cornstarch
- 1 teaspoon lemon juice
- 3 tablespoons strawberry jam
- Red food coloring

Decoration:

- Red and white love heart candies
- 4 fresh strawberries

Directions

1. First we make the sponge cake. This recipe is for a 22 cm tin. It's best to bake the dough without the basket or on the grill pan.
2. Put the sugar, eggs and salt in a bowl. Mix at the highest speed for 10 minutes. Spoon the flour little by little into the airy mixture. Grease the spring form, spoon in the mixture and bake at 155°C for 25 minutes. The sponge cake is ready when golden brown in color and it springs back after touching.
3. To make the yellow cream, slice open the first vanilla pod and scrape out the seeds. Put the milk in a pan and add the vanilla pod and seeds. Bring the milk slowly to the boil. Turn the heat down low and let the vanilla infuse the milk.
4. Meanwhile, whisk the egg yolks together with the sugar until creamy. Then carefully spoon in the corn starch. Remove the vanilla pod from the milk and remove the pan from the heat. Add a little of the hot milk to the egg mixture and stir well. Pour it in the remaining milk and bring to the boil, stirring. Let it cook gently for 5 minutes and keep stirring so the cream doesn't burn. Sieve the cream, leave to cool and set aside in the refrigerator.
5. Place a piece of plastic wrap over it to stop a yellow skin from forming.

Lemon Meringue Pie

Servings 8 persons

Ingredients

For the dough:

- 30 g powdered sugar
- 65 g sugar
- 30 g ground almonds
- 250 g flour
- 125 g butter (room temperature)
- 1 egg
- 1 pinch of salt
- 1 vanilla pod
- For the filling:
- 100 ml lemon juice
- Grated peel of 2 lemons
- 300 g powdered sugar
- 300 g butter

- 3 egg yolks
- 2 eggs
- For the meringue:
- 200 ml egg whites (approximately 8)
- Vinegar
- 200 g sugar
- 160 g powdered sugar
- For decoration:
- Cape gooseberry
- Lemon
- Spun sugar
- Yellow food coloring

Directions

1. Weigh out the ingredients for the dough. Mix the butter with the sugar and the ground almonds. Cut the vanilla pod in two halves and use a knife to scrape out the seeds. Mix the vanilla with the egg, salt, flour and sugar until homogeneous. If you have a food processor, you can let it do the work. Wrap the dough in plastic wrap and leave in the refrigerator for an hour.

2. Now for the lemon cream. Melt the butter at a moderate heat and add the lemon juice and zest. Then add the powdered sugar, stir well and briefly bring to the boil. Beat the eggs and egg yolks. Remove the pan from the heat and mix the eggs together with the butter, sugar and lemon until smooth. Place the pan on the heat and keep stirring, so that the egg does not solidify. Pass the mixture through a fine sieve into a bowl. Cover the bowl with plastic wrap and leave for at least one hour in the refrigerator. If you've made more cream than in the recipe, for example, double the amount, it will need longer to set.

3. For the meringue, weigh out all the ingredients. Put a few drops of vinegar on a paper towel and degrease the mixing bowl. Put the egg whites in the bowl and whip until stiff while you slowly add the sugar. Sift the powdered sugar into the beaten egg whites and beat a little more. Put the egg whites in a piping bag.

4. Remove the dough from the refrigerator and roll it out to about half a centimeter thick. Take a loose bottomed cake tin that fits in your Airfryer and grease. Place the dough in the tin, press down well and prick some holes. If you have baking beans you can use these, putting a sheet of parchment paper on the dough then the beans on top. Heat the Airfryer to 160°C and bake the casing for 30 minutes.
5. For the meringue, weigh out all the ingredients. Put a few drops of vinegar on a paper towel and degrease the mixing bowl. Put the egg whites in the bowl and whip until stiff while you slowly add the sugar. Sift the powdered sugar into the beaten egg whites and beat a little more. Put the egg whites in a piping bag.

Cranberry Muffins

Servings 4 persons, Preparation time 10 minutes, Cooking time: 15 minutes

Ingredients

- 75 g flour
- 1½ teaspoons baking powder
- 1 teaspoon cinnamon
- 3 tablespoons sugar
- 1 small egg
- 75 ml milk
- 50 g butter, melted
- 75 g dried cranberries
- 8 paper muffin cups

Directions

1. Preheat the Airfryer to 200°C. Double up the muffin cups to form fou cups in total.
2. Sift the flour into a bowl and add the baking powder, cinnamon, suga and a pinch of salt. Mix well.

162

3. In another bowl, lightly beat the egg and add the milk and melted butter. Mix well. Stir this mixture into the flour. Then add the cranberries and mix.
4. Spoon the batter into the doubled muffin cups and carefully place them in the fryer basket.
5. Slide the basket into the Airfryer and set the timer to 15 minutes. Bake the muffins until they are golden brown and done. Let the muffins cool in the cups.
6. Variations: Replace the cranberries with: -75 g blueberries -75 g chopped apple mixed with 1 tablespoon lemon juice -75 g chopped dates with 1 tablespoon orange juice -100 g pure chocolate (70% cocoa) with 1 tablespoon grated orange peel
7. Savory Muffins: Replace sugar and cinnamon with 50 g grated cheese and add one of the following to the batter: -75 g boiled ham in strips with 2 tablespoons finely chopped parsley -75 g coarsely chopped and roasted hazelnuts, pistachios or pecans

Chocolate Cake

Servings 8 persons, Preparation time 15 minutes, Cooking time: 30 minutes

Ingredients

- 3 eggs
- 125 ml sour cream
- 150 g flour
- 150 g caster sugar
- 125 g unsalted butter
- 40 g cocoa powder
- 1 tsp baking powder
- ½ tsp bicarbonate of soda
- 2 tsp vanilla essence
- Chocolate icing:
- 150 g chocolate
- 50 g unsalted softened butter
- 200 g icing sugar
- 1 tsp vanilla essence

Directions

1. Preheat the Airfryer to 160°C.
2. Place all the cake ingredients into a food processor and mix well. Transfer to the oven dish.
3. Place the oven dish into the basket of the Airfryer. Slide the basket into the Airfryer and set the timer for 25 minutes. Once the time is up and the timer rings, prick the cake with a wooden skewer or fork. If it comes out clean, the cake is cooked through. If it's still sticky, place the cake back into the Airfryer and set the timer for another 5minutes.
4. Remove the dish from the basket and leave the cake to cool on a wire rack.
5. Meanwhile, melt the chocolate au bain marie or in the microwave. Leave to cool a little, then mix all of the icing ingredients together.
6. Remove the cooled cake from the oven dish and place it onto a plate. Cover with the chocolate icing and serve.
7. You can replace the bicarbonate of soda with baking powder if necessary. You can also mix the cake batter by hand; the preparation time will be slightly longer.

Crème Brûlée

Servings 4 persons

Ingredients

- 2 vanilla pods
- 250 ml whipped cream
- 250 ml milk
- 10 eggs
- 100 g sugar
- 70 g super-fine sugar
- Garnish:
- 2 tablespoons brown sugar candy
- 2 tablespoons super-fine white sugar
- Blueberries
- Redcurrants
- Spun sugar (if desired)

Directions

1. Pour the cream and milk in a pan. Cut open the vanilla pods and scrape the seeds out. Add to the cream and milk. Also add the vanilla pods, because they still give flavor. Heat the mixture on a medium heat (almost to boiling) and stir regularly with a whisk.
2. Take two bowls. Break the eggs and separate the egg yolks from the egg whites. You don't need the whites. Beat the yolks with a whisk and add the granulated sugar and white super-fine sugar. Mix carefully, but don't make it too frothy. Remove the vanilla pods from the milk and cream and pour the warm mixture into the beaten yolks, constantly stirring. Let the mixture rest for approximately 20 to 30 minutes.
3. Fill the oven dishes with the mixture. Cook the crème brûlées for 50 minutes at 90°C. You can test how it's set by shaking the dish gently. Let them cool fully.
4. Mix the granulated sugar and brown sugar candy in the blender or mincer. You now have the ideal sugar mixture for the crunchy layer. Sprinkle a fine layer of sugar on each dish and caramelize the sugar using a small kitchen blowtorch. The sugar should melt and caramelize, but must not burn.
5. Garnish the crème brûlées with the berries or whatever else you feel like.

Brownies

Servings 9 persons, Preparation time 20 minutes, Cooking time: 30 minutes

Ingredients

- 200g butter
- 100g dark chocolate
- 100g white chocolate
- 4 small eggs
- 200g sugar
- 2 tablespoons of vanilla extract
- 100g flour
- 150g pecan nuts, chopped
- 1 cake tin 20 x 20 cm, greased

Directions

1. Preheat the oven to 180°C Melt half of the butter with the dark chocolate in a thick-bottomed pan, and melt the white chocolate in another pan with the rest of the butter. Leave to cool.

2. Using the mixer, beat the eggs briefly with the sugar and vanilla. Divide the flour into 2 portions and add a pinch of salt to each.
3. Beat half of the egg-sugar mixture through the dark chocolate. Then add in half of the flour and half of the nuts and mix. Do the same with the white chocolate mixture.
4. Pour the white and brown brownie mixture into two different sides of the cake tin. Use a spatula to partially mix the two colours, creating a swirl. Bake the brownies for about 30 minutes. When ready, the surface should be dry to touch.

Cherry Clafoutis

Servings 4 persons, Preparation time 15 minutes, Cooking time: 25 minutes

Ingredients

- 200 g fresh cherries or 1 jar of cherries, well-drained
- 2-3 tablespoons crème de cassis or vodka
- 50 g flour
- 2 tablespoons sugar
- 1 egg
- 125 ml sour cream
- 10 g butter
- Powdered sugar
- Small, low cake pan, 15 cm diameter

Directions

1. Pit the cherries and mix them in a bowl with the kirsch or crème de cassis.
2. Preheat the Airfryer to 180°C.

3. In another bowl, mix the flour with the sugar, a pinch of salt, the egg and the sour cream until the dough is smooth and thick. Add a drop or two of water, if necessary.
4. Spoon the batter into the buttered cake pan. Place the cherries evenly over the top of the batter and place the remaining butter in small chunks evenly on top.
5. Put the cake pan in the fryer basket and slide the basket into the Airfryer. Set the timer to 25 minutes. Bake the clafoutis until it is golden brown and done.
6. Immediately after baking, dust the clafoutis with plenty of powdered sugar. Serve the clafoutis lukewarm in slices.

Chocolate Cake 2

Servings 6 persons, Preparation time 10 minutes, Cooking time: 25 minutes

Ingredients

- 50 g soft butter
- 50 g fine granulated sugar
- 1 egg
- 50 g flour
- 1 tablespoon cocoa
- 50 g pure chocolate, in pieces
- 1 small cake pan (volume 400 ml), buttered

Directions

1. Preheat the Airfryer to 160°C.
2. In a mixing bowl, beat the butter and sugar with a mixer for approximately 5 minutes until light and creamy.
3. Add the egg and beat into the butter. Then add the flour, cocoa powder and a pinch of salt. Mix thoroughly. Finally add the jam, the chocolate pieces and the grated orange peel and mix well.
4. Transfer the batter to the cake pan and use a spatula to smooth the surface.

172

5. Put the cake pan in the fryer basket and slide the basket into the Airfryer. Set the timer to 25 minutes and bake the cake until it is nicely browned and done. The cake is done if a tooth pick inserted in the center of the cake comes out dry.
6. Let the cake cool in the pan for 5 minutes. Then turn the cake out onto a wire rack to cool.
7. TIP: Make the cake one day ahead of time and store the cooled cake tightly wrapped in plastic wrap. This makes the cake even more delicious.
8. Variations:-Lemon Cake: Replace the cocoa and the chocolate with the juice and grated peel of half a lemon.- Vanilla Cake: Replace the cocoa and the chocolate with the scrapings of half a vanilla pod.- Chocolate Ginger Cake: Replace the chocolate pieces with 2 tablespoons finely chopped candied ginger.

Apple Pie

Servings 8 persons

Ingredients

For the dough:

- 125 g butter or margarine
- 125 g superfine sugar
- 250 g self-rising flour
- Salt
- ½ lemon

For the filling:

- 1.5 kg tart apples
- 60 g golden raisins
- 10 g currants
- 2 tablespoons vanilla custard
- 5 tablespoons apricot jam
- 200 g sugar
- Pinch of cinnamon

For decoration:

- Powdered sugar

Directions

1. Clean the lemon, grate the peel and squeeze the fruit. Mix the butter with the sugar, the lemon juice, the lemon peel and a pinch of salt until combined. Then rub the self-rising flour into the butter mixture.
2. Peel and slice the apples. Mix with the raisins, currants, custard, apricot jam, cinnamon and sugar.
3. Roll the dough out to 28 cm (for one tin in the Airfryer XL) or divide into three and roll out to 20 cm each (for three tins in the regular sized Airfryer). Grease the tin(s) with a little melted butter and place a sheet of parchment paper on it/them. Put the dough in the tin and press down level. To avoid air bubbles, prick holes in the base with a fork. Spread the filling on top and bake the cake. The cooking time and temperature for the regular Airfryer is 30 minutes at 160°C; for the XL, 50 minutes at 160°C.
4. Allow the cake to cool in the tin and sprinkle with powdered sugar.
5. Regular sized Airfryer: 3 spring form cake tins (16 cm) Airfryer XL: 1 spring form cake tin (20 cm) Parchment paper

Apricot and Blackberry Crumble

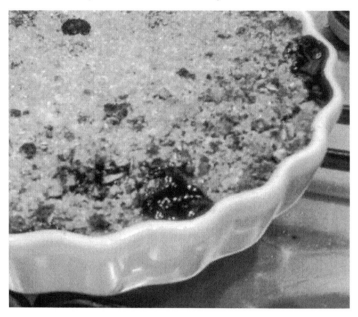

Servings 4 persons, Preparation time 10 minutes, Cooking time: 20 minutes

Ingredients

- 250 g fresh apricots
- 75 g sugar
- 100 g fresh blackberries
- 1 tablespoon lemon juice
- 100 g flour
- 50 g cold butter, in cubes
- Shallow, round cake tin, 16 cm diameter

Directions

1. Preheat the Airfryer to 200°C.
2. Halve the apricots and remove the stones. Cut the apricots into cubes and mix them in a bowl with the lemon juice and 25 g sugar.
3. Grease the cake tin and spread the fruit mix over the tin.

4. In a bowl, mix the flour with a pinch of salt, the remainder of the sugar, the butter, and 1 tablespoon cold water until it is more or less consistent and then turn it into a crumbly mixture using your fingertips.

5. Distribute the crumbly mixture evenly over the fruit and press the top layer lightly.

6. Put the bowl in the basket and slide the basket into the Airfryer. Set the timer to 20 minutes and bake the crumble until golden brown and done.

7. Serve the crumble hot, lukewarm, or cold with ice cream, whipped cream, or vanilla sauce.

8. TIP: Apples, pears, mangos and peaches are also suitable for making crumbles, and they are delicious in a combination with raspberries, blueberries, or fresh cranberries.

Apples with Almond Stuffing

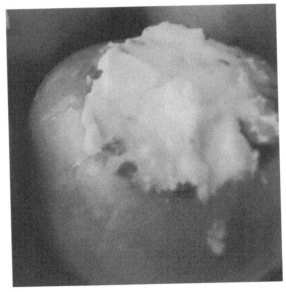

Servings 4 persons, Preparation time 10 minutes, Cooking time: 10 minutes

Ingredients

- 4 small, firm apples
- 40 g blanched almonds
- 25 g (white) raisins
- 2 tablespoons sugar
- Vanilla sauce (see tip) or whipped cream
- Parchment paper

Directions

1. Wash the apples and remove the cores.
2. Grind the almonds in the food processor and add the raisins, sugar and calvados. Turn the mixture another 30 seconds in the food processor.
3. Preheat the Airfryer to 180°C. Line the bottom of the basket with baking parchment, leave 1 cm of the edge open.

4. Fill the apples with the raisin mixture and put them side by side in the basket.
5. Slide the basket into the Airfryer and set the timer to 10 minutes. Bake the apples until brown and done.
6. Serve the apples on plates and spoon the vanilla sauce or ice cream next to the apples.
7. TIP: Vanilla sauce; Heat 125 ml whipping cream with the scrapings from one vanilla pod and 2 tablespoons of sugar for 2-3 minutes. Stir to dissolve the sugar. Leave the sauce to cool before serving.
8. TIP: Stuffed Peaches with Amaretti; Halve two peaches and fill them with a mixture of four crumbled amaretti cookies, 1 tablespoon slivered almonds, and 1 tablespoon finely chopped ginger balls. Roast them in the same way as the apples.

Orange Chocolate Fondant

Serves 4, Preparation time 15 mins, Cooking time 28 mins

Ingredients

2Tbsp Self Raising Flour

4Tbsp Caster Sugar

115g Dark Chocolate

115g Butter

1 Medium Orange (rind and juice)

2 Medium Eggs

Directions

1. Preheat your Airfryer to 180°C.
2. Grease four ramekins.

3. Melt the chocolate and butter in a glass dish over a large pan of hot water. Stir until it is a nice creamy texture.
4. Whisk and beat the eggs and sugar until they are pale and frothy.
5. Add the orange along with the egg and sugar mixture into the chocolate. Finally stir in the flour and combine everything evenly.
6. Fill the ramekins 75% full with mixture and bake for 12 minutes.
7. Remove from the Airfryer and allow to cook in the ramekins for 2 minutes. Turn the ramekins upside down (gently) onto a serving plate tapping the bottom with a blunt knife as this will loosen the edges.
8. The fondant will release from the centre and you will have a lovely pudding with a soft centre.
9. Serve with vanilla ice cream or caramel sauce.

Mini Pumpkin Pies

Serves 9, Preparation time 15 mins, Cooking time 15 mins

Ingredients

1 Pumpkin Pie Filling (see my recipe link above)

75g Plain Flour

33g Butter

15g Caster Sugar

Water

Directions

1. Preheat your Airfryer to 180°C.
2. Start by making your pastry – place the plain flour and butter in a mixing bowl and rub the fat into the flour. Add the sugar and mix well. Add the water until the ingredients are moist enough to combine into a nice dough. Knead the dough well until it has a smooth texture.
3. Grease your pastry cases with butter.
4. Roll out your pastry and cover the cases of your pastry moulds.

5. Fill to 80% full with pumpkin pie filling.
6. Place in your Airfryer and cook on 180°C for 15 minutes.
7. Leave to rest for five minutes and then using a butter knife remove the pies from the casing and leave on a cooling rack to cool.

Unit Conversions

Grams to ounces

Example:

1000g converted to ounces

$\frac{1000g}{28.35}$= 35.27 ounces

Degrees celcius to degrees Fahrenheit

Example:

100°C converted to degrees Fagrenheit

100°C×1.8+32= 212°F

About the author

I am a South African citizen and I love my country. However, we are faced with many hardships in Africa. We all strive to help each other and improve our country. I am an engineering student and I write kindle books in my spare time. I enjoy writing short, informative books that provide useful information that is to the point. Your support is much appreciated.

Made in the USA
San Bernardino, CA
16 April 2016